Give Your
HEART
a Good Spring Cleaning

Choose to...
Give Your
HEART
a Good Spring Cleaning !

* *

Throw Away Trash,
Give Away Treasures, and
Keep What's Important

Kendra Smiley

Kendra Smiley

(John 8:32)

VB
VINE
BOOKS

SERVANT PUBLICATIONS
ANN ARBOR, MICHIGAN

Vine Books is an imprint of Servant Publications especially designed to serve
evangelical Christians.

To protect the privacy of some of the individuals whose stories are told in this
book, names and characterizations have been fictionalized, although they are
based on real events. With permission, real names and events are portrayed in
stories of close friends and family members.

Published by Servant Publications
P.O. Box 8617
Ann Arbor, Michigan 48107

Cover design and illustration: Hile Illustration and Design, Ann Arbor, Michigan
Back cover photo courtesy of Pam McComb of McComb Photography, 7114
Webster St., Landover Hills, MD 20784.

02 10 9 8 7 6 5 4 3 2

Printed in the United States of America
ISBN 1-56955-147-2

LIBRARY OF CONGRESS CATALOGING-IN-PUBLICATION DATA

Smiley, Kendra, 1952-
Give your heart a good spring cleaning / Kendra Smiley.
     p.   cm.
  ISBN 1-56955-147-2 (alk. paper)
  1. Christian life Anecdotes.   I. Title.
BV4517.S6   1999
248.4—dc21   99-22347
                                                    CIP

Dedication

This book is dedicated to John—
who through the years has helped me determine what to
Throw Away, what to Give Away, and what to Keep.

Contents

Acknowledgments

When I read a book, I always start at the very beginning—way before the text begins. I read the title page and the dedication and I never pass over the acknowledgments. I have always imagined that the folks named in this section were the true heroes. And I was right.

It is with love and a great big smile that I thank my husband, John. He has provided both inspiration and perspiration for this and every project I have ever tackled. He is my number one motivator, encourager, proofreader, and dishwasher. I don't deserve him, but I do appreciate him.

Thanks also to our sons, Matthew, Aaron, and Jonathan. They have generous spirits and loving hearts (and they are also very funny!). Thanks, guys, for letting me share pieces of your lives.

Thank you to all the people in my physical family and my church family who "filled the gap" for me while I was super-glued to the chair in front of the computer. A special thanks to Pam, who filled more than her share of gaps. She is a wonderful part of my life and a gift from God.

A big thank-you to my editor Kathy Deering, my publicist Kolleen O'Meara, and to Bert Ghezzi and Don Cooper at Servant for all the encouragement and professional guidance. You are wise teachers.

And finally, thanks to you, the reader of this list of kudos. Thanks for caring about your spiritual life and development enough to buy a book encouraging you to give your heart a good spring cleaning!

Introduction

Mom's Plan and My Heart

A s the saying goes, in spring a young man's fancy turns to thoughts of love. Although I'm not certain exactly what a "fancy" is, I think it is safe to admit that in spring my fancy turns to thoughts of spring cleaning rather than love.

Clutter Attack

I want to be quick to point out that I am never overly pleased by these thoughts, and that it is not necessarily the season that precipitates them. I'd hate to blame the lovely weather or harness it mercilessly to my cleaning urges. Occasionally these thoughts occur in the summer, fall, and winter, too. More than the calendar, my thoughts of spring cleaning are activated by an attack of clutter in my life.

"I know the screwdriver is in the drawer by the refrigerator. If you can't find it look under the coupon collection, the prolific pen and pencil pile, the warranties, and the guarantees!" I holler in reply to the urgent request from my teenage son. "It's in there somewhere."

That one line, "It's in there somewhere," uttered with great hope from my sighing lips, can many times motivate me to consider cleaning my drawers, shelves, and closets. I want to be quick to point out that step one—"considering" the cleaning activity, "thinking" about the clutter, or "contemplating" the process—is much more pleasant than actually doing the work. Far too many times I get stuck at that very important first step and never get on to the actual work.

Mom's System

It's not that I come unprepared or untrained for the task of spring cleaning. When I was young, my mother made sure I developed the lifetime skills to handle the clutter of accumulation. In fact, it was typical for my mother to enter my bedroom the very first day of summer vacation with three empty boxes and a big black crayon. The boxes were never the same size but rather graduated sizes—small, medium, and large. Mom would announce that my job for the day (or however long it took) would be to sort through everything in my room, a project I fondly referred to as dejunking. At that point she would take her crayon and label the large box "Throw Away." The medium-sized box always got the label "Give Away" and the smallest one, "Keep." I was never sure why Mom wasn't able to find three boxes of the same size, but it didn't seem to bother her.

After the labeling was complete, I started the job. I went through every drawer, every shelf, and every hanger in the closet. Each item I handled had to go into a box. Throw Away, Give Away, Keep. Where did each item belong? The plan was simple and very effective, yet it was always plagued by two serious problems. Actually, they were two very serious and difficult questions, questions that hovered over the entire dejunking and cast their dark shadows on the process.

Difficult question number one: What if I throw this item away and then discover that I need it?

I know that this is a terrifying thought for many of you, especially those of you who are the self-appointed archivist for any group to which you may belong. Who will keep all the old newsletters and minutes if you don't? Who will store the programs from past presentations and functions, the slips of paper too precious to destroy?

Or perhaps you maintain the official storehouse for vacation Bible school paraphernalia. Who will stock the used Popsicle sticks and the frozen orange juice can lids if you don't? Is there anyone else willing to dedicate an entire drawer in the kitchen to house these valuable VBS raw materials? What if you throw these items away and you (or anyone else in the four-county area) discover you need them?

Equally difficult question number two: What if I keep this item and it is only junk?

If that is the case, you will continue tripping over the clutter until you dejunk again. And if you are a skilled procrastinator (or have very extensive storage), that might not be for years and years!

These two questions always complicated the process of cleaning my room. They did not, however, keep me from doing it. Mom made sure of that. Early each summer for as far back as I can remember, I started and completed the dejunking task. Eventually I was married and no longer brought stuff into my mother's home. Instead I filled my own shelves, drawers, cubbyholes, and closets.

The years passed and I became the mom. As distasteful and demanding as I might have felt my mother's dejunking system was, I found myself using precisely the same routine when I was the one in charge. One day several years ago I had moved forward in the cleaning process from contemplation to actual work. As I began the task and emptied the contents of the drawer by the refrigerator, my mind began to wander.

Dejunk Your Life

"I wonder if I can use this same simple system to dejunk my life?" I asked myself. "Can I empty the contents of my heart, my mind, and my memory and sort through the clutter? Are there things to throw away? Do I have things inside of me that I can give away? What should I keep?"

Although my dreaming slowed the cleaning process that day, I realized that Mom's plan had great potential for dejunking not only the drawer by the refrigerator but also my life. For years my home had benefited from her system, and I was beginning to believe that the drawers, shelves, and cubbyholes of my heart, mind, and memory could benefit from it too! So the process began, the process of sorting through the clutter inside of me, sifting through the things I'd been storing, and putting each item into the appropriate box. Throw Away, Give Away, Keep. I began the spring cleaning of my heart.

Why don't you join me in the personal dejunking process? Grab three boxes of your own and a big black crayon. Take a look inside yourself and let's see if we can decide on the correct box for each item.

Chapter 1

Let's Throw Away False Guilt

First, I picked up my imaginary Throw Away box. When I was a girl cleaning my bedroom, the Throw Away box was always the biggest ... but I usually managed to fill it. Would the same prove true during my heart-cleaning project?

Was there anything inside of me—in my heart, mind, or memory—that I could put into the Throw Away box? Did I have garbage I had been tripping over or lugging around that could be eliminated? Upon examination, I realized that the answer was yes. I found several things that definitely needed to go. One was labeled "Guilt."

It is no wonder to me that people talk about being on a guilt trip. The word picture is perfect if you imagine the baggage that you have packed for other trips. Unpacking from a guilt trip may not be easy, but those bags may carry things that should be in the Throw Away box.

The Power of One Small Word

Many things have been known to cause me guilt, from credit cards to an unused treadmill. Children are capable of producing guilt. So are jobs, husbands, mirrors, telephones, candy bars, state police cars, and even the word *no*. As diverse as these items are, they and many others can all produce guilt (varying in intensity from mild to crippling).

Let's take a look at one small word. When you were a child, chances are great that the word *no* was one of your favorite and most powerful weapons. Why, I've even known children who will say "no" when they really want to say "yes"—just to show that they can!

"Do you want an ice-cream cone?" asked Sally's mom.

"No," Sally replied immediately, only to quickly add, "Well, maybe yes."

Then something mysterious happens as we age. We find it more and more difficult to say "no," especially when asked if we can do something good.

"Can you make another four dozen cookies for the teacher-appreciation day at school?"

"OK."

"Will you be on the decorating committee for the retreat?"

"All right."

"I need a substitute teacher for Sunday school. Can I count on you?"

"I suppose."

We somehow forget how to say "no" even though it used to be our favorite word. I have decided that this riddle is linked to the type of question that is asked. No one ever asks you to do something bad. If someone were to inquire of you, "Do you have time to be an ax murderer? I think you'd do a great job," you would immediately answer "No!" But no one asks you to do something bad; they ask you to do something good. It's not "will you be an ax murderer?" but "will you bake more cookies?" So we say yes.

A friend who attended a seminar shared with me one of the gems that she heard that day. The speaker declared, "When you say yes to something, you say no to something else." It is possible to say yes to a good thing and no to something better or best. Gina, a busy mother of four preschoolers, agreed to make forty vests for the children's Bible club. She had said yes to a "good thing."

"But as I sat at my sewing machine making Bible vests for other children," she admitted, "I found myself screaming at my own kids."

It's possible she should have said no, even though she might have had to deal with the guilt of using that word. But guilt can become clutter many of us trip over. It is heavy baggage that can potentially be carried throughout our lives.

Two Kinds of Guilt

So do we throw guilt into the Throw Away box as soon as it is discovered? Not necessarily. It has been my experience that there is bad guilt (bound for the Throw Away box) and good guilt (to be examined, handled, and eliminated by an admission of wrongdoing and a change in behavior). Bad guilt, also called false guilt, results when there has been no intentional wrongdoing. Good guilt occurs when we have intentionally or irresponsibly acted in a wrongful way. Bad guilt always belongs in the Throw Away box. Good guilt (caused by our conscience and our knowledge of right and wrong) must be handled another way.

These two varieties of guilt are not always easy to distinguish. One indispensable tool in the process is honesty. "Then you will know the truth, and the truth will set you free" (Jn 8:32). When you discover guilt cluttering up your heart, the first step is to be honest about the situation. I wish being honest was as easy to actually do as it is to acknowledge.

We attend a small rural church. It is a wonderful, loving church that is as close to family as I can imagine. Since our average attendance is about one hundred, special events and programs do not always produce huge turnouts. Our family is supportive of most activities.

Currently we have one son in college, one son in high school, and one son in junior high. Each of our two older sons is on his school's football team. On one busy autumn weekend we traveled to a nearby town on Friday evening and watched our high school son play football. Then on Saturday morning I left home at about 5:00 A.M. to drive to a women's retreat where I was speaking. At the conclusion of the retreat, I drove to our son's college and joined the rest of the family for the evening game.

Occurring simultaneously to the college game was a special program at church. A speaker had been scheduled for an evening session, and we missed it.

On Sunday morning I inquired about the program held the night before and found that it had been poorly attended.

"Well," I thought, somewhat defensively, "we had a football game on our schedule. Maybe other people had things that were important too."

Bam! I was hit smack in the heart by a load of guilt. It was heavy baggage, and I knew I didn't want to carry it around for long. I started the dejunking process ... right there in Sunday school class. I knew I had to be truthful so that I could determine if it was bad guilt (and destined for the Throw Away box) or good guilt that I could learn from.

Before you jump to my defense and pitch it all in the Throw Away box, I have to admit two things. First, our son was a "walk-on" on the college team and hadn't been to enough practices yet to be in uniform for the game. Second, I really didn't want to go to hear the speaker. His topic was a good one but it just didn't appeal to me. With those pieces of information, you have probably completely shifted loyalties and are ready to assume that I was feeling all good guilt. I'm not sure that's true either.

What was the truth? The truth was twofold. Number one, I did not have a desire to attend the seminar and the family outing was a legitimate excuse. Number two, I was not personally responsible for the success or failure of the program. I had not indicated that I would be in attendance or encouraged the committee to select that particular date.

So what about the guilt? Was it good or bad? In this instance, I decided that it was bad guilt. I committed no intentional wrongdoing. Out it went in the Throw Away box.

The Goods on Good Guilt

What if I had prayerfully determined that it was good guilt, that I had intentionally or irresponsibly done wrong? Let's go back to the guilt-producing word *no* for just a minute. Last summer I received a phone call.

"Kendra, we need one more teacher for vacation Bible school," Sandie said. "Would you be able to teach fifth and sixth graders?"

For some reason, that day at that moment, it was not difficult to say no. I looked at my calendar and the week of VBS was pretty full, plus I had already agreed to lead the worship. Surely they could find someone else to teach.

"I don't think I'll be able to do it," I said with no guilt initially.

"Would you mind praying about it?" she asked. "I don't need an answer right away."

Often that phrase is enough in itself to stimulate guilt, but Sandie's request was not manipulative in the least. She was genuine in her desire for me to pray. So I did, and I discovered (almost immediately) some good guilt associated with my negative answer. I was actually being selfish, thinking it must be someone else's turn. When I realized the truth (not by what Sandie said, but through prayer), I called her back and said I'd teach the class. I had good guilt that the truth had revealed, and I was able to change my behavior.

What Gives Us the Guilts?

But saying "no" isn't the only thing that can produce guilt. Our own kids can cause us guilt too.

"When the baby was born," one of my girlfriends once confided, "I got seven pounds of baby and fourteen pounds of guilt!" According to her it was standard equipment, not an option. I can attest to that. I am the baby in my family and as a teenage girl I did very little baby-sitting. In fact, I can remember only one time. I watched the daughter of one of the high school coaches. The preschooler was nice and didn't really give me any problems at all; however, upon returning home that evening I distinctly remember telling my mother that there *had* to be an easier way to make money! As far as I was concerned, mowing lawns was a better job.

Then came Matthew. He was our first son, born after six years of marriage. (John always said that we had to wait until I grew up. Thank goodness we didn't wait *that* long.) I'll always remember his first bath. I had the instruction sheet from the hospital in hand—the gospel as far as I was concerned. The poor kid almost froze to death as I analyzed every step and direction. To make it worse, my mother, my older sister, and my aunt were all there for the momentous occasion. My mother and sister alternated between giving directions and feeling genuinely sorry for poor Matthew. Even my aunt got into the act and told me what to do, and she had never had children! Do you think I experienced guilt? I didn't want to be the first one in the family to inadvertently freeze her child to death.

"I must be a terrible mom!" I lamented to myself. The

truth? I wasn't a terrible mom. ("Love covers a multitude of sins" … and a lack of skills.) I was just a very inexperienced one. So I needed to persevere and gain that experience; I was not purposefully doing wrong. Matthew survived my feeble attempts at mothering a newborn. I always say that I practiced on him and the other two boys reaped the benefits. I stand on my record of not freezing one child.

"But, Mom …"

In addition to the guilt caused by newborns, our older children can dish it out. Most of them soon discover that guilt is a great source of motivation and manipulation.

"Mom, *everyone* has those jeans!"

"I *need* these $175 tennis shoes."

"Why can't I go to the unchaperoned boy-girl party? Give me *one good reason.*"

Statements like these, in one form or another, have been effective guilt-producers for years and years. But what is the truth in each statement? Should they produce bad guilt (into the Throw Away box) or good guilt (a change in behavior)?

"Mom, *everyone* has those jeans!"

Tilt! When someone uses the word *everyone, all, never,* or *always* … take cover. Those words are seldom (did you notice I didn't say never?) accurate. John and I have a dear friend who is a pastor. In the early days of his ministry, he would say things such as, *"Everyone* is upset because we moved the piano."

"Specifically, who is upset?" John would ask.

"Mrs. Jones." John would remind him that Mrs. Jones was one person (albeit one noisy person) and not "everyone."

Everyone does not have those jeans. That is the truth. There should be no good guilt generated by that line.

"I *need* those $175 tennis shoes."

The truth of the matter is that there are very few things each of us actually needs. Check the definition of the word *need*. We need water and food and shelter and clothing. There are many things we want but very few things we need. No good guilt here either.

"Why can't I go to the unchaperoned boy-girl party? Give me *one good reason*."

One evening we heard exactly this question and statement from Matthew. He was in the eighth grade and we had set the standard that there would be no attendance at private boy-girl parties in junior high. He was allowed to attend school functions, and those, combined with youth group activities at church, provided him with plenty of socialization.

Matthew is typically a nonemotional debater. He operates on logic of a sort and hopes that he can ultimately outlast you in a debate. "Why can't I go? Give me *one good reason*."

Well, our reasons, presented at the top of our open stairway, were not sufficient for him. As we stood in front of our bedroom door and he stood in front of his, the debate continued until my husband said, "I have a pretty good idea of what might happen at an unchaperoned boy-girl party. Would you rather stay home or have to call us to get you when something inappropriate happens?"

After a long pause, our son's answer came: "Fine." The

translation for that word in our home is "discussion finished." That was it. The truth was presented and I felt no guilt.

The next morning at breakfast, our second son, just in sixth grade at the time, spoke up. "Oh, by the way," Aaron began, "when I'm in junior high you won't need to give that boy-girl party speech. I heard the whole thing through my bedroom door last night." (I felt no guilt there either.)

Mouths of Babes

There are times, however, when we can experience good guilt from our kids. When our youngest son, Jonathan, was a preschooler I received a phone call one day that totally preoccupied me for at least thirty minutes. When I eventually said good-bye and walked into the living room I was shocked. Jonathan had taken every single toy out of the toy box and off the shelves and had scattered them all over the room.

Because he is my third child (those of you with only one child, please take my word for this), I was able to inhale slowly and actually give him some instruction. (My firstborn would have been in deep trouble immediately.) "Well," I said slowly and deliberately. "You have a real mess here. What I want you to do is to pick up all of these toys and put them away."

"I'm too busy," he replied. "I'm not going to pick up my toys nany more times."

I inhaled again and tried to imagine that I had not heard that reply. "What did you say?" I asked in disbelief, giving him the opportunity to change his tune.

"I'm too busy," he repeated, oblivious to the imminent danger. "I'm not going to pick up my toys nany more times."

At this point all I could think about was where did he get that belligerent attitude, and when did *Sesame Street* start teaching the phrase "I'm too busy"?

Well, maybe he hadn't heard it on *Sesame Street.* Maybe he heard me say it once or twice (or multiple times). Good guilt landed smack dab in my heart, but I didn't let it govern the immediate situation. Inhaling again, I continued the conversation. "Well, Jonathan, I can see how a guy like you might be too busy," I admitted. "I get busy myself sometimes. So I'll just pick up these toys for you and give them away to some little boy who isn't as busy."

Jonathan thought about the option for just an instant and then replied, "You could give them away to Aaron. He has to share with me!"

Pretty clever, huh? I want you to know that Jonathan did end up picking up the toys and we did not have to give them all away to Aaron. And I ended up taking a close look at my choices for busyness and making a concerted effort not to be too busy for the important things—like Jonathan.

And On It Goes

As our children become adults, they do not lose their ability to foster guilt. A woman in her seventies told me that recently her daughter came to her with a complaint. She let her mother know in no uncertain terms that Mom had let her down decades before.

"There were many times," the daughter said, "when you

missed the ballgames when I was cheering. As a mother myself, I realize how important my attendance is at those events."

As the older woman told me the story, she admitted that there were definitely games she missed, but she wondered why her daughter didn't remember when she took the time to dye all the cheerleaders' shoes or when she hosted the annual sleepover. Mom experienced guilt, dished out by her offspring.

Parents are capable of guilt giving too. As I prepared to deplane from a recent trip, I overheard a conversation between the two gentlemen in the seats behind me. "I usually travel on Sunday or Monday, but I'm flying in a day early for this trip," said one of them.

"Why is that?" asked his seatmate.

"To see my parents and do my yearly duty," he replied. "Guilt, you know."

Family of all ages can cause guilt, and the false guilt needs to be put into the Throw Away box. The good, genuine guilt can be a motivation for change as we admit the intentional or irresponsible behavior, ask for forgiveness, and change the behavior.

Mirror, Mirror

A mirror can cause guilt too. Some of you are nodding your heads in agreement, admitting that it has been two weeks or more since you cleaned the bathroom mirror. I understand that accumulated grime and toothpaste fingerprints can cause guilt, but that is not the "mirror guilt" I am referring to.

There is a mirror we look into to compare ourselves with others. This is never a good idea, for comparison often leads to jealousy or to a self-defeated attitude. I look into the mirror and see my inability to play the piano well. I should have practiced more. When I compare that to my brother's ability or to Sue's or Rhoda's, I come up short. I'm just not as good. I compare and I come up short; guilt and other negative emotions result. "I should be better at remembering other people's birthdays. Barb is so much better than I am." "Why can't I seem to get to choir practice on time? Ken is always there early. I should be more diligent about arriving early."

I compare and I don't measure up. I look in the mirror and my reflection doesn't look as good as yours. I accumulate guilt as I note one way and then another that I miss the mark. What is the truth? Well, the truth is that I typically compare my weaknesses to someone else's strengths. The contest is rigged. I'm destined to lose and to feel guilty.

My boys coined a phrase that is very appropriate in helping me appreciate the truth of the mirror. They like to say, "Always remember, you are unique, just like everyone else." Funny and true. We *are* all unique. Have you ever heard people whine about their birth order? She complains that she is the eldest, for they do all the work. He wishes he were not the middle child because he's always overlooked. She would rather not be the baby; after all, the baby is never taken seriously. Have you felt this way?

Because of the nature of reproduction, there was only one moment in history when you could have been created. If you were not the eldest in the family (or the middle or the baby), you would not *be* at all. In fact, if your mother and father had been fighting that evening and had reconciled one day later, the child that was conceived would not have been you. You *are* unique!

So is it bad guilt or good guilt when we look in the mirror and come up short? It is bad guilt if you compare your negatives to someone else's positives. It is good guilt if you are doing some timely self-examination and discover an area where improvement is needed. All the bad guilt goes into the Throw Away box. The good guilt requires an admission of wrong-doing, a request for forgiveness, and a change of behavior.

Apology Accepted?

When my children were very young, they discovered the manipulative power in the words "I'm sorry." They learned that, when I caught them in an offense, they could utter those two words and I would grant them an instant reprieve. That was the case until I realized that they did not actually mean they were sorry. Their behavior had not changed.

When it dawned on me that these words were insincere and used merely to get me off their backs, the jig was up.

"Matthew, quit chasing Aaron," I said.

"I'm sorry," he replied.

"No, you're not," I countered. "If you were sorry you would stop."

"I'm sorry" is an empty phrase without a change in behavior, a change in direction, a repentance. Years ago I saw an acquaintance that I hadn't seen for quite awhile. As we sat and drank a soft drink together, he began to pour out his life story since we last saw one another.

It was not a pretty picture.

His wife had kicked him out of their home. His children were estranged from him. He was struggling to keep his job. Oh, yes, and he was having an affair. All the trouble had begun, according to this man, after his wife discovered he was committing adultery.

As he poured out this barrage of information, he kept saying, "I'm sorry. I'm just so sorry."

Finally I had heard more than enough of the gruesome details, and I abruptly presented him with a question. "Jim," I said, "are you sorry that you committed adultery and lost your family or are you sorry that you got caught?"

Jim had obviously never thought about that question before. Finally he answered in all honesty. "I guess I'm sorry I got caught," he replied.

If he was experiencing any guilt at all (and I'm not sure he was), it was good guilt. Guilt has the potential to help us admit our wrongdoing, ask for forgiveness, and change our behavior. It is also important that we forgive ourselves. If we fail to do that, we carry around bad guilt that belongs in the Throw Away box.

After they [Paul and Silas] had been severely flogged, they were thrown into prison, and the jailer was commanded to guard them carefully. Upon receiving such orders, he put them in the inner cell and fastened their feet in the stocks.

About midnight Paul and Silas were praying and singing hymns to God, and the other prisoners were listening to them. Suddenly there was such a violent earthquake that the foundations of the prison were shaken. At once all the doors flew open, and everybody's chains came loose. The jailer woke up, and when he saw the prison doors open, he drew his sword and was about to kill himself because he thought the prisoners had escaped. But Paul shouted, "Don't harm yourself! We are all here!"

ACTS 16:23-28

The guard was an instant victim of guilt. The prison doors were open and he assumed that the prisoners were gone. His guilt was so overwhelming that he decided to take his own life. It was only the shout from Paul that spared him. The guard was experiencing bad guilt. He had not done anything wrong, either intentionally or irresponsibly, and the bad guilt was so powerful that it almost killed him.

Most bad guilt is not that overwhelmingly powerful, but it can be destructive in small increments, gnawing away at the person who keeps it in his or her heart. All bad guilt belongs in the Throw Away box.

"Let us draw near to God with a sincere heart in full assurance of faith, having our hearts sprinkled to cleanse us from a guilty conscience and having our bodies washed with pure water" (Heb 10:22).

Reflection

Look inside of your heart. It is time to do some spring cleaning. Do you see any guilt? Write down what is causing you guilt.

What is the truth about the situation?

In light of the truth, is it bad guilt or good guilt?

Pitch the bad guilt into the Throw Away box. If it is good guilt, admit your wrongdoing, ask for forgiveness, change your behavior, and forgive yourself.

Chapter 2

Let's Throw Away Forgiven Sins

After I sorted through the guilt inside of me, I quickly discovered another goody for the Throw Away box—sins I had repented of and for which I had received forgiveness. Wait a minute, I thought, if I had genuinely repented—that is, turned around from sinful behavior—and asked for and received forgiveness from God, what were these things doing inside of me? Talk about clutter!

That's a great question and the answer isn't an easy one. Maybe you are like me. I realize that I have done something wrong—"for all have sinned and fall short of the glory of God" (Rom 3:23)—and I admit my wrongdoing. Then I ask God to forgive me, for I know that "if we confess our sins, he is faithful and just and will forgive us our sins and purify us from all unrighteousness" (1 Jn 1:9).

God is more than happy to forgive me when I have truly repented, but many times I don't forgive myself. So days, maybe weeks, later I find the remembrance of those same old sins haunting me and I ask once again for forgiveness. The Bible says that God forgives us and that He also forgets our sins: "I, even I, am he who blots out your transgressions, for my own sake, and remembers your sins no more" (Is 43:25). I imagine the conversation going something like the following.

"Lord," I say apologetically, "I am so sorry for what I did. I know that I've asked you before, but I am asking again. Please forgive me."

"I'm sorry, Kendra," God replies kindly and gently, "but I have no recollection of what you are talking about." He doesn't remember because He has already given me forgiveness.

Shop Talk

Forgiveness is ours because Christ paid the price for our sins. When I think of paying, I think of shopping....

As I entered one of my favorite dress shops, I immediately noticed the rack marked "Clearance." Clothes on clearance shout, "Try me on. Take me home."

I rummaged through the rack and saw a very cute skirt that was just my size. There was a blouse too—and a sweater. I scurried into the tiny dressing room, where, in solitude, I judged whether or not the ensemble was attractive and calculated the discount to see if the items were really a deal. As it turned out, it was a good shopping day. Everything fit and the prices were definitely right.

With a hint of satisfaction, I took my purchases to the woman at the cash register. Using an old-fashioned system, she listed each piece of clothing on a carbon-backed receipt: one skirt, one blouse, one sweater. Then she totaled the debt I owed and, when I handed her my check, wrote, "Paid in full" on the receipt. I got a copy and so did she.

My store debt was paid in full by the rendering of money. My sin debt was paid in full by the rendering of Christ's blood. But with the latter transaction, there was no receipt, no carbon-backed paper listing all the times I had fallen short. I have no record of my sins nor do I need one because God forgives, pays in full, and does not desire a receipt. He keeps no record of my wrongs. How unlike God I am.

Just Dessert?

About ten years ago John and I taught a class on marriage at our church. One evening all of the couples went out to dinner, after which we piled into a couple of vans and headed for an ice cream shop for dessert. All the women stayed at the picnic tables while the men went to the window to order. When they returned, John had failed to get the treat I had requested. He had inadvertently substituted something much more fattening.

For some lame reason, I reacted very poorly to the mistake. Somehow it became a big deal in my mind (probably because I had already eaten a week's worth of fat grams and calories during dinner). I told him that he had delivered the wrong dessert! I don't specifically recall his response, but he was no doubt gracious to me. Within seconds, I realized how rude I was being, apologized, and accepted his gooey, sweet offering.

He seemed to have no problem accepting my apology and went on visiting with the other couples. I, on the other hand, was immediately miserable. I had embarrassed John and myself and was ashamed of my self-centered behavior. My pride also entered the picture and I inwardly declared myself the least qualified to teach others about marriage. No one else really seemed to care; no damper on the party was evident—only the one I was imposing on myself.

When we returned home I again apologized to John and he reassured me that it was no big deal. I also asked God to forgive me for my self-centered attitude and for my pride. My repentance was genuine. The next morning, however, I felt just as miserable as I had the night before.

"How could God forgive me?" I questioned. "He expects more from me as a teacher. I know I have let Him down."

My repentance turned to repetition, as again and again I asked God to forgive me. "But how could He?"

In the midst of my self-pity and indulgence the phone rang. Sharon, a friend of mine for many years, was on the line. She and I had not talked for almost four years, but our families always exchanged cards at Christmas and stayed connected.

"Hi, Kendra," she began. "This is Sharon. I know you must be surprised to hear from me."

"I sure am," I replied, "but what a treat! What's happening?"

"Well," she began, "this morning in my prayer time you came to mind so I prayed for you. Then the strangest thing happened. I knew that God wanted me to call you with a message."

As soon as she said that, I grabbed a pen and a pad of paper. I knew Sharon and had observed her walk with Christ for many years; she was not someone to contrive a message from God. If Sharon had a message for me from God, I wanted to get it all down.

"He wanted me to tell you He loves you. Isn't that wild? I know you know that," she continued, "but I couldn't get it out of my mind that I was supposed to call. That's it."

"Thanks, Sharon," I said with more gratitude than she realized. "Have a great day!"

Sharon had no idea what I had been thinking. She had no reason to believe that I had doubted God's love for me. She didn't know a thing. She merely chose to respond to God and be obedient, and I was so thankful that she did. God loved me. That was exactly the reminder I needed. God knew my heart and had forgiven me. He was even willing to help me forgive myself.

The Cross Is Central

My friend Penny had been asked to communicate God's message of repentance and forgiveness at a women's retreat. In preparation, she had her husband construct a life- (and death-) sized cross, which she used as a focal point. She spoke on the reality of sin, the importance of repentance, and the victory over sin that we could have because of the sacrifice of Christ.

"Ladies," she said, "this cross is empty. Jesus left the cross in order to make room for our sins. Now we must choose to admit our sins, repent, and nail them to the cross." She then provided paper, pen, nails, and a hammer and encouraged her audience to prayerfully give their burdens to Christ and symbolically and literally nail them to the cross.

"Why nail them?" I asked.

"Because the nails made it much harder for them to reclaim those burdens," she replied.

God in a Box

Maybe it is difficult for me to accept God's forgiveness because I know that I am not so generous with my forgiveness. I then try to put God into a human-sized box so that I can understand Him better. I try to limit Him, as I am limited. But putting God into a box is always risky business because He will never stay in a box we construct for Him. He will not be limited by our limited knowledge of Him. "'For my thoughts are not your thoughts, neither are your ways my ways,' declares the Lord. 'As the heavens are higher than the earth, so are my ways higher than your ways and my thoughts than your thoughts'" (Is 55:8-9).

When God is put into a box, He explodes from it because a box defines and limits but God has no limits. He is sovereign. He can do anything He wants to do. "Our God is in heaven; he does whatever pleases him" (Ps 115:3). God is capable of forgiving a sinner who repents. He forgives and forgets even when that is difficult for me. All of those sins I have repented of and received forgiveness for need to be put into the Throw Away box.

Do you not know that the wicked will not inherit the kingdom of God? Do not be deceived: Neither the sexually immoral nor idolaters nor adulterers nor male prostitutes nor homosexual offenders nor thieves nor the greedy nor drunkards nor slanderers nor swindlers will inherit the kingdom of God. And that is what some of you were. But you were washed, you were sanctified, you were justified in the name of the Lord Jesus Christ and by the Spirit of our God.

1 CORINTHIANS 6:9-11

Reflection

Are there remembrances of forgiven sins that are cluttering your heart? Now is the time to accept God's forgiveness and toss them into the Throw Away box.

If you have not repented or turned from those sins, that is the all-important first course of business. Do it now!

Chapter 3

Let's Throw Away Hurts and Disappointments

The Throw Away box was filling up. Good thing that it was the biggest box. As I surveyed the stuff remaining in my heart, I suspected I still had a few more items to toss out.

How about hurts, both the real ones and the imagined ones? I had a few of those that I was allowing to clutter my heart.

Hurts in All Sizes

Hurts take many different shapes and forms. Hurts can be fresh and new, or they can be almost as old as we are. Hurts can be based on facts, or they can be based on feelings. With so much diversity, what do these hurts have in common? They all cause pain to the person carrying them in his or her heart, mind, or memory.

Recently I joined a team of speakers at a seminar. I enjoyed working with this talented group and getting to know them a little better. One of the women, Carol, was especially fun to be with. We shared the life experience of raising teenage boys, so it was entertaining and reassuring to exchange stories on the pleasures and perils of motherhood.

On the second day of the conference, Carol called home and listened to the messages on her answering machine. Before she had left town, she had made carpooling arrangements to transport her son to a special sporting event. One of the messages on her machine was from the prearranged driver, announcing that something important had unexpectedly come up and she would not be able to drive. Carol, who was many miles from her home, listened to the message in disbelief. How could the woman back out of the agreement? Why would she choose to do something so unkind? Carol's emotions were high as she told me about the phone call.

We immediately began to discuss possible solutions to the transportation dilemma, but before long Carol blurted out her deeper concern. "Why would that woman want to hurt Ben or me?" she demanded tearfully. "Why would she be so mean?"

Carol knew she had to be creative (and quickly) in order to solve the problem. But more than the obvious stress of this challenge, she was overwhelmed by feelings of hurt and disappointment. In Carol's thinking, the would-be driver had purposefully hurt her and her son.

Carol was tucking the hurt into her heart. It didn't matter whether the woman intended to hurt her or (more likely) whether the hurt was unintentional. Carol had picked up something that she would have to sort through before long. The hurt would have to be thrown away at some point.

It Doesn't Really Matter

Dawn and I sat together at the game. We were both mothers of high school seniors. Their upcoming departure for college became our topic of conversation.

"I'll really miss Nick," Dawn said with a sigh. "He has such a good perspective on life. When I get my feelings hurt by something insignificant, he is always the first to remind me that it isn't worth it."

That can be so true. Many of the hurts we allow to clutter our hearts are very petty. But petty or not, if we choose to give them the space in our hearts, minds, and memories, they add to the clutter.

I remember standing up from my spot in the bleachers after a very disappointing Little League baseball game. My son Jonathan had played a great game, as had the other boys on his team, but they hadn't been able to score in the last inning. They were defeated.

"Oh, boy," I whined. "They did such a good job. If only they could have had another inning to catch up. I think they could have done it." I continued my lament until finally my oldest son decided that I had moaned long enough.

"Mom," Matthew said, "you have to keep this in perspective. Is anyone going to hell because Jonathan's team lost? If not, it isn't all that important."

He was right. Perspective is important.

Welcome In

As ridiculous as it sounds, I have even invited hurts into my life. Well, it's not like I sent out a formal invitation or anything; I just structured the situation so that the hurt hit me smack in the middle of my heart.

Let me give you an example. My friend Sue is an excellent pianist. Through the years she and I have cooperated on many musical programs for children. My musical ability is not in her league, but I can usually make up for it with enthusiasm. After one particularly exciting program, I grabbed (figuratively speaking) the first audience member who wandered by the piano.

"Wasn't that wonderful?" I said with exuberance and genuine appreciation for the talent of the children.

"Well," she replied, "I didn't really like the middle part. I thought it was rather slow and boring."

I wanted to scream, "How could you not think that these children were adorable in every single part? What are you, a blind and deaf Scrooge?"

Fortunately I just nodded my head in no particular direction and immediately looked for Sue. I told her about my hurtful encounter, one which I had brought upon myself, and sought comfort from this kindred spirit. I had gone fishing for a compliment and had caught a big fat hurt!

That day, at that moment, Sue and I made a pact. Whenever either one of us felt the need for a boost, for a compliment from another person, we vowed that we would be there to comply. From that point forward, every time I asked, "How do you like my dress?" she would answer with an affirming statement. (I always like "It makes you look thin.") From then on, if she asked, "What do you think about my haircut?" I would reply with a compliment. (She prefers "It makes you look younger.")

We realize that we might not be telling the whole story, but this pact was designed for desperate moments, times when one of us really needs a boost. Furthermore, we agreed that, after an appropriate amount of time, if we needed to adjust or amend our first responses that was fine. Our pact will help keep hurts from ever entering.

Keeping Score

As mothers, we typically multiply our opportunities to feel hurt by the number of children we have. I believe that the umbilical cord is never actually cut. It just stretches a *really* long way!

As a stable adult, I am baffled when I realize that my heart has collected not only my own hurts but also those of my children. These hurts need very frequent sorting, for children are quick to forgive. It is not uncommon for a mother to continue to foster a child's hurt long after the child has extended forgiveness. I have known mothers who keep score in their children's lives long after the children have torn up the score card.

Women are notorious scorekeepers. Many years ago I was in charge of soliciting help for a community event. "Hi, this is Kendra," I said as I called a potential recruit. "I am calling to see if you could be on the kitchen committee."

"Who else is on the committee?" the woman replied.

I began to read the list and was abruptly stopped when I read a certain name.

"Oh, I can't be on that committee if so-and-so is on it. You see, thirty years ago so-and-so did such-and-such," she concluded.

Initially I marveled at this woman's memory. Then it hit me: it would have been better if she had forgotten the such-and-such that so-and-so had done because that long-ago offense had caused a hurt. How sad. She had never thrown that hurt away.

Have you ever had a bad week with someone close to you? Consider Linda and her husband, Tim.

On Monday Tim didn't carry the garbage cans out to the curb. On Tuesday he forgot to pick up milk from the store, even though he said he would. On Wednesday he announced that he was responsible for cookies for the monthly office coffee break. ("Didn't I mention that before?") On Thursday he told Linda he'd be playing golf on Saturday morning. (If he lived that long.)

All week long Linda took in those little hurts, smiled like a saint, and was agreeable. Until Friday. Tim called to say that they would have to postpone their evening out because his boss expected him to pick up a package across town.

That was it! Linda had had it! The straw had broken the camel's back and she exploded. "What do you mean you *have* to pick up the package?" she screamed into the receiver, completely aware that the volume could permanently damage Tim's hearing. "We have a date scheduled."

As Tim recovered from the explosion and caught his breath to respond, Linda unloaded the rest of the clutter that had hurt her that week. "And I'm sick of you playing golf! Bake your own cookies next time. I'm obviously not important to you.

You can't even remember to pick up milk or take out the garbage!"

By now poor Tim was desperately struggling to get his bearings. What did milk and cookies have to do with the package he must retrieve? And where in the world did the garbage come in?

Throw Away the Score Card

Women *are* accomplished scorekeepers. We have logged the hurts (real or imagined) of our lives and, when we deem it the appropriate time, we dump the entire load on the offender.

This is a combination of putting throw-away items into the Give Away box (more about this in later chapters) and taking part in an exercise in futility. The truth of the matter is that, on any particular afternoon, most people do not remember what they had for lunch much less how they have inadvertently hurt or offended someone earlier in the week. Keeping score is not healthy or profitable. Instead, it is much better to throw away those hurts as soon as we can. In Linda and Tim's case, each day probably warranted a discussion to keep the clutter of hurt to a minimum.

God's Word says that love "keeps no record of wrongs" (1 Cor 13:5). It keeps no record of the sins of which we or others have repented. Love does not keep score by accumulating and logging the hurts in life. Instead, love puts those hurts into the Throw Away box. It doesn't matter if the hurts are intentional or unintentional, real or imagined, they are all candidates for that large box.

"Bear with each other and forgive whatever grievances you may have against one another. Forgive as the Lord forgave you" (Col 3:13).

Reflection

Do you have any hurts from the past that you have been storing? Identify them and put them into the Throw Away box.

Are there hurts that you are keeping for someone else, such as your children? Identify those and unload them too.

Do you tend to keep score? Make the choice to handle the hurts sooner and not let the clutter accumulate.

Chapter 4

Let's Throw Away Arrogance and Selfishness

I was ready to quit. This Throw Away box was wearing me out! The dejunking of my heart, mind, and memory was taking awhile, but I was making progress.

As I continued the spring cleaning, I discovered some nasty stuff inside of me. It reminded me of the peanut butter sandwich that I had stashed on the shelves with my comic books when I was a girl. When I was dejunking my room, I came across that moldy surprise. On the one hand, it was disgusting enough to make me want to resign from the job. On the other hand, it reminded me how necessary the dejunking was.

Well, I did not find a moldy PB&J in my heart, but I did discover things that were just as disgusting, including arrogance and selfishness. I wasn't sure when those things were added to the clutter, but I was sure there was no place for them.

The Paradox of Pride

Arrogance, sometimes called pride, can be such a paradoxical thing. Usually I find it rearing its ugly head when there has been no particular performance to take pride in. It is almost as though, by assuming the posture of pride, I try to convince the world that I have done something I can take pride in.

God's Word tells us, "Do nothing out of selfish ambition or vain conceit" (Phil 2:3). An arrogant and prideful person does most things out of these two motivations.

I remember discovering the verse above. Isn't it wonderful when a piece of Scripture jumps off the page at you and you are convicted? Well, maybe "wonderful" doesn't describe the initial feeling I have when God's Word reprimands me, but that is the eventual goal.

"Do *nothing* out of selfish ambition or vain conceit" (emphasis mine). How did God know that I had just volunteered for a project with both motivations? I read the verse and knew that, in this area, arrogance and pride were my problems. The project I had volunteered to do had beautifully masked my ulterior motives, but God snatched away the mask through His Word. I was convicted.

What did I need to do next? I knew that the arrogance and pride belonged in the Throw Away box and, if necessary, I would resign from the project to assure that I had no improper motives. I prayed and asked God for forgiveness. I repented and told Him of my willingness to forgo the project that I had undertaken for my own gain.

God knew my heart and saw my repentant attitude; through a series of extraordinary events, He arranged for me to stay with the project. Each time I worked with the group, I would silently remind myself that *nothing* was to be done from selfish ambition or vain conceit. *Nothing* was to be done in arrogance or pride. Before too long, my attitude toward the assignment had genuinely changed and I began to serve.

When the project was complete, God chose to open an unbelievable door of opportunity for me. I had allowed His Word to change my attitude from selfish ambition to service, and He had created a blessing for me. It doesn't always happen that way. But it can only happen that way when we obey.

Up in the Air

John entered pilot training seven days after we were married and flew on active duty for three years after that. At that point there was a respite from the cockpit as he taught school. After two and a half years, John began to pursue a flying position in the U.S. Air Force Reserves. He became an intelligence officer but still had the desire to fly again. After all, he was trained. He was qualified. He wanted to fly.

Each month at his reserve weekend, he would attempt to initiate the change from desk to cockpit, but nothing ever materialized. His ambition was not strong enough to make it happen. Then, on one particular reserve weekend, he spent his travel time to the base specifically praying about his desire to fly. The culmination of his conversation with God was a relinquishment of that dream of flying again.

"I want what You want, Lord," he said. "If it is Your desire that I never fly again, that is my desire. I give You my flying. I don't want it or anything else more than I want Your will in my life."

When John arrived at the base that day, he was greeted by the group commander, who miraculously asked him if he was still interested in flying. And fly he did for the next twenty years. It doesn't always happen that way, but it can. "Do *nothing* out of selfish ambition or vain conceit." Put arrogance, selfishness, and pride into the Throw Away box.

It's Your Call

On another occasion, it was my turn to face God about my career. "It's for you, Kendra," said John as he handed me the phone.

"We have made our decision about the teaching position," said the voice at the other end of the line, "and we have decided to hire the other applicant."

"Thank you," I said politely, holding back the tears. "I appreciate your call." Then I hung up the phone and cried. And cried and cried and cried. How awful! I didn't get the job. Now what would I do? I found it hard to believe that the other candidate was more qualified. What could I do now? I didn't want to substitute teach. I wanted to have my own classroom. I deserved my own classroom.

But God's Word told me, "Do *nothing* out of selfish ambition or vain conceit." Throw it away. Shove the arrogance into the Throw Away box and go sign up as a substitute teacher. I did just that and became a regular at the local junior high. Five weeks into the school year, the junior high girls' physical education teacher (who had become my lunch buddy) posed an interesting question.

"Are you still looking for a job?" she asked.

"Well," I replied with a smile, "I've stopped actually looking because we are five weeks into the school year. But I'm still interested."

"Did you know that there is an opening in Potomac?" she asked.

"I don't even know where Potomac is," I said.

"It's not too far from here and I know that they are looking for a fourth grade teacher," she continued.

"That's terrific! Do you think I can get an interview?"

"I know you can! The principal is my brother."

And off we trotted to the school office, where she called and arranged an interview for that evening. By midnight I had the job. It doesn't always happen that way, but sometimes it does.

Operating out of Disobedience

What if we hang on to our arrogance and pride, to our selfish ambition or vain conceit? Then we operate out of disobedience, something that is never a good idea. I know. I have made that mistake.

Not too long ago I had an opportunity to clean more of the clutter of arrogance from my heart. Cliff is a retarded man who lives in the small community where I worship each Sunday. The church I attend is the largest one in town; actually, it's the only church in town.

In the spring of the year, Cliff began showing up for worship. At first he stayed outside the building and listened. Then, because of the friendship that had developed between Cliff and our pastor, he came inside. Before too long, Cliff was arriving for the 10:15 service before 8:00. The praise band assembled at 8:00 each Sunday to rehearse for the morning worship. Our pastor plays a guitar in the band, so Cliff felt that he was welcome too.

For weeks Cliff wandered around the sanctuary while the band practiced. There are three guitars, one keyboard, an omnichord, a flute, and a trumpet. Oh, yes, and two vocalists, Linda (who really can sing) and me (again compensating with enthusiasm). My job also included manipulating the transparency on the overhead projector. One morning as we played through our songs, Cliff became fascinated with the projector. He sat right beside it with his legs hanging over the podium and watched as I changed the transparencies each time we started a new song.

After several weeks of this, Cliff asked me if I could use his help. "Sure," was my reply and I handed him the next transparency. After each song Cliff handed me the sheet that had been on the screen and I handed him the new one. When the practice ended Cliff would resume his wandering, landing in the pastor's class in the sanctuary for Sunday school and sitting in the most remote corner for church.

Sunday after Sunday Cliff manipulated the overheads as the praise band practiced. Before long he was taking all the songs for the morning and laying them on the altar rail in order. Then he put them on and took them off as each song began and ended. One Sunday after practice I asked Cliff if he would like to help during the worship service. His face lit up and he readily agreed to help. So Cliff became the official praise band transparency man. I was not sure if he was able to read; this job seemed like a delightful stretch for him.

Cliff, who is a very large man, would sit with his legs dangling over the podium and do an impeccable job of aiding the congregation in worship each week. When the pastor called for the congregation to greet one another, Cliff would turn off the machine, shake my hand, and find his way to his remote corner of the church.

It happened that way for weeks and weeks. Then one Sunday, as we greeted one another and the praise band disassembled, Cliff chose to sit in a different pew—mine.

Please do not act shocked to hear me call it "my" pew. I know that most of you have your pews too. That is the spot where my family sits each week. We are joined many times by teenagers who do not have family in the church and occasionally by other visitors. But Cliff had never joined us before. He had literally moved from the spot farthest from the lectern to the spot closest, for we sit in the second row.

"Wait a minute," I thought in my arrogant heart. "You are taking up a lot of space that I might need." Nevertheless, I slid in beside him and the service continued. I think the sermon was good that morning, but I'm really not sure. Most of the hour I spent cleaning out the ugly arrogance I had discovered in my heart and putting it into the Throw Away box.

Up to that point, knowing Cliff had not put any demands on me. It had not inconvenienced me or made me feel uncomfortable. It had been easy to be kind in those circumstances. Now he had chosen to invade my space. At first I decided that I would be pleasant but would do nothing to encourage Cliff's move. As I momentarily pondered that strategy I realized the prideful feelings I had and I was ashamed.

Asking God for forgiveness, I also realized that I was being called to throw away my arrogance and give away encouragement (precisely what I had initially decided *not* to do). Later in the service, when the pastor asked for the sharing of joys and concerns, I knew what God wanted me to do.

"Pastor?" I said raising my hand. "I am thankful for Cliff's help during praise time. He does a great job."

I turned to look at Cliff and he was smiling from ear to ear. I may have gained a permanent pew partner. So be it. Hanging on to pride and arrogance is never the best choice. If you find those things in your heart, put them into the Throw Away box. "For by the grace given me I say to every one of you: Do not think of yourself more highly than you ought, but rather think of yourself with sober judgment, in accordance with the measure of faith God has given you" (Rom 12:3).

Arrogance in Ages Past

Now the whole world had one language and a common speech. As men moved eastward, they found a plain in Shinar and settled there.

They said to each other, "Come, let's make bricks and bake them thoroughly." They used brick instead of stone, and tar instead of mortar. Then they said, "Come, let us build ourselves a city, with a tower that reaches to the heavens, so that we may make a name for ourselves and not be scattered over the face of the whole earth."

But the Lord came down to see the city and the tower that

the men were building. The Lord said, "If as one people speaking the same language they have begun to do this, then nothing they plan to do will be impossible for them. Come, let us go down and confuse their language so they will not understand each other."

So the Lord scattered them from there over all the earth, and they stopped building the city. That is why it was called Babel—because there the Lord confused the language of the whole world. From there the Lord scattered them over the face of the whole earth.

GENESIS 11:1-9

These folks wanted to make a name for themselves, motivated by selfish ambition and vain conceit. They had aspirations that were not pleasing to God. Their arrogance and selfishness belonged in the Throw Away box.

Reflection

Look into the clutter in your heart. Is there any arrogance? Are you pursuing something for selfish ambition or vain conceit? Then put it into the Throw Away box.

Many times we are most selfish in our closest relationships. Take a good look at your heart. Do you find any selfish behavior infiltrating your deepest friendships? Are you selfish in your relationship with your husband? Are you demanding with good friends and family? Do not let familiarity breed selfishness.

Chapter 5

Let's Throw Away Anger

The Throw Away box was very full, but I knew that I had at least one more thing that could be added. I had thrown away false guilt, forgiven sins, hurts and disappointments, and arrogance and selfishness, but the process of dejunking my heart, mind, and memory needed to include throwing away anger.

Anger? *Moi?* Did I really discover that I had anger mixed with all the other clutter I had been sorting? A few years ago, I would have answered no. I would have wholeheartedly denied the possibility that I had any anger inside of me. After all, I never hit or kicked things and I was never guilty of throwing something at another person. Weren't those the signs of anger? Didn't it take those aggressive actions to indicate the presence of anger?

Throwing Bowls and Words

I once knew of a woman who, in my opinion, had a definite problem with anger. In contrast to me, she *did* throw things. In fact, in a fit of rage, she once threw an "unbreakable" bowl at her husband. He ducked and it missed him, but it hit the brick fireplace and broke. She then had the audacity to send the pieces of the bowl to the manufacturer and ask for a replacement. After all, it was supposed to be unbreakable, wasn't it? (I guess she decided that throwing a bowl at your husband constituted normal use.)

"Like a city whose walls are broken down is a man who lacks self-control" (Prv 25:28). She was an angry woman. But did I really have anger inside of me? Yes, I had to admit I did. The key difference between the agitated bowl buster and me was that I had learned to express my anger in a socially acceptable manner. The anger inside of me was evidenced not by flying place settings but by flying sarcasm. Truthfully, I am not certain which of the assaults could do more damage—the physical one or the more subtle, verbal attack.

As a young child I found sarcasm to be a safe way to express my anger. I was angry about my father's alcoholism, angry about my family's choice to ignore the issue, and angry that this unidentified curse dictated my life. I also knew how to behave and that the overt signs of anger were not allowed. So I stifled the easy, more natural reactions and went with sarcasm.

As a Christian today, I would tell you that I feel strongly that sarcasm is very destructive and has no place in my interactions. It is a form of anger I had to put into the Throw Away box.

Recently I was the recipient of someone else's anger that wore the mask of sarcasm. I was introduced to a woman whom I had been looking forward to meeting. She was a speaker and I had had the pleasure of hearing her speak just months before.

"It is such a treat to meet you," I began. "I heard your opening message at a Christian college recently and I really appreciated your words. I was unable to stay into the afternoon so I missed your second session." As soon as the words were out of my mouth, I regretted saying them. No speaker wants to hear that his or her message was preempted by something else. My genuine compliment had turned sour with the addition of the last sentence.

Unfortunately, the speaker chose to react to that last sentence rather than the opening, encouraging remarks. "You left before I spoke again?" she smartly quipped. "That's good to know. Well, I'll have to see if there is a workshop on healing being offered today."

Ouch, I got the point. My stupid words were rewarded with her sarcasm and anger. I suffered only a flesh wound and the recovery was almost instantaneous. But the lesson was loud and clear: Kendra, don't allow your sarcasm to wound someone else.

The Sullen Approach

Maybe you have never thought of yourself as an angry person. Maybe you, too, have learned to express anger in a socially acceptable manner. If sarcasm isn't your weapon of choice, perhaps it is sullenness. A pouter seldom gets tagged with the angry label, but that kind of behavior might be an indicator that there is anger in the clutter.

I once heard a commentator on the radio say that anger invisibly chained the angry person to the one with whom he was angry. That's similar to what we used to tell our son Jonathan. When he was growing up, before he got just as tall as his older brothers, they took pleasure in teasing him. It was nothing serious and nothing mean, but they enjoyed seeing if they could get him to react.

"Jonathan," his dad and I would say, "the big boys are just trying to pull your chain. All you have to do is ignore them and they'll stop."

Although there was great truth in that statement, I must admit that, looking at it from Jonathan's standpoint, it might have been easier for him to ignore me than his older brothers. The advice (though difficult to accept and apply) was correct. His anger invisibly chained him to the perpetrators. They were able to make him react because of his anger. He was the marionette; they were the puppeteers.

How does the same principle work for adults? Imagine that you are out on Saturday morning, running errands and doing a little shopping. It is almost noon so you decide to treat yourself to your favorite sandwich at a fast-food restaurant. As you pull into the parking lot, lo and behold, there sits Bonnie's car. *She* is inside. Boy, you really don't want to see her. She has made you so mad lately.

"That takes care of the sandwich," you think as you pull out of the lot.

You drive to the restaurant down the street and settle for second choice. Who won? Who was in charge? You or Bonnie? Who got to eat the good sandwich?

Anger chains you to the one with whom you are angry. And

who wants to be chained to *that* person? If you have anger inside, throw it away. Don't get confused about which box to put your anger into. Putting it in the Give Away box (see chapters 7–12) isn't a good choice. God's Word says, "In your anger do not sin" (Ps 4:4; Eph 4:26). Everyone has feelings of anger. Acting on those feelings by violent action, sarcasm, pouting, or any other behavior done with the desire to hurt another person is sin.

Who Feels Better?

There was a knock on Georgia's door one evening. It was Mary, a woman from her church. Mary had a determined look as she asked if Georgia had a minute to speak with her.

"Sure," Georgia replied. "Do you want to come in?"

"No," said Mary with her jaw set and her face looking very stern, "this won't take long."

And then the tirade began. Mary explained that she had been seeing a counselor to deal with some of the "issues" in her life. According to Mary, the counselor had listened intently for weeks as she poured out her feelings of inadequacy, anger, and resentment. The week before, the counselor had given Mary an assignment—one that he guaranteed would make her feel much better. She was to confront anyone and everyone with whom she was angry and tell them exactly what was on her mind.

Tonight was Georgia's turn. After her introduction, Mary proceeded to aggressively unload her anger on Georgia, turning her anger into a verbal weapon. There was no forgiveness expressed, just the expression of the right to hurt Georgia because of the anger her various actions and their perceived intentions had precipitated.

Needless to say, the confrontation was not done in love. Mary was simply giving away the anger and resentment she had been carrying. Did this confrontation make Mary feel better as her counselor had promised? Well, I suppose it did, but I liken Mary to a person carrying around a large bag of garbage.

The bag she is carrying is getting heavier and smellier by the moment. To find relief, Mary goes to Georgia's home and dumps it all out. Mary feels better and has gotten rid of the garbage, but Georgia now has it all over her front porch and she must do the cleaning up.

Dumping your anger upon someone else—putting it into the Give Away box—is not appropriate or healthy. And if my analogy holds true, it can be very messy! Does that mean that a confrontation is never appropriate? It is inappropriate if it is done from a desire to hurt someone who has hurt you (or you think has hurt you) or if it is done to force that person to apologize. If you have experienced forgiveness—in the words of Dr. Archibald Hart, "a surrendering of your right to hurt a person who has hurt you"—it is possible to confront in love. When the confrontation is done in a loving way, you are not giving away garbage.

A Special Tree

Ken lived in the church's parsonage. It was a little two-story bungalow about twenty-five feet from the church building. In fact, it was tucked in the L that was formed by the sanctuary and the education wing, so it was twenty-five feet from the church on both the north and east sides.

The only tree that shaded Ken's home was a walnut tree, a beautiful, sturdy tree that he estimated to be over seventy years old. He enjoyed the shade this tree provided in the summer months and liked to watch it shed its colorful leaves and grow new ones as the seasons changed.

One day someone decided that the old walnut tree was a lawsuit waiting to happen. Why, what if someone tripped on a walnut and sued the church? The negative publicity for the tree was rapidly spreading and before long, the church board decided they would have to cut it down.

Ken was angry. He was very angry. How could those people think that it was the right decision to destroy that beautiful walnut tree? Did they realize how barren his yard would become when the tree was gone? Ken decided that he was too angry to confront. He was afraid that he might say something he would regret.

As he realized that he was unable to change his circumstances, he had a thought of how he might turn his anger into something good. He asked the church committee if he could have a portion of the trunk when the tree was cut down. And with this large and crude piece of wood he started the task of turning anger into beauty.

Ken split the wood and he chiseled it. He carved it and sanded it and formed it into a splendid work of art. He made a magnificent harp, a beautiful work of art and of music. He fashioned this instrument and then began the task of learning how to play it.

I heard him play one day. He explained to those listening that he had only begun to master playing with his right hand and that his "left hand wasn't ready yet." He sat with that exquisite instrument in his hands, that instrument fashioned from the zeal of his anger, and played "Jesus Loves Me."

Ken took his anger and threw it away. When the anger was gone there was room for the beauty of the harp and his song. Getting rid of anger and putting it into the Throw Away box makes room for better things ... things that we can give away.

> Now Abel kept flocks, and Cain worked the soil. In the course of time Cain brought some of the fruits of the soil as an offering to the Lord. But Abel brought fat portions from some of the firstborn of his flock. The Lord looked with favor on Abel and his offering, but on Cain and his offering he did not look with favor. So Cain was very angry, and his face was downcast.
>
> GENESIS 4:2b-5

At this point, even though Cain had not followed God's instruction for offerings, he had the option to throw away his anger. In fact, God encouraged him to do just that.

> Then the Lord said to Cain, "Why are you angry? Why is your face downcast? If you do what is right, will you not be accepted? But if you do not do what is right, sin is crouching at your door; it desires to have you, but you must master it."
>
> GENESIS 4:6-7

God encouraged Cain to master the sin that he was embracing. God wanted him to do what was right and to throw away his anger. Unfortunately, Cain did not choose to put his anger into the Throw Away box. Instead he chose to give it away. Cain killed his brother Abel: "Now Cain said to his brother Abel, 'Let's go out to the field.' And while they were in the field, Cain attacked his brother Abel and killed him" (Gn 4:8).

God and His Word encourage us to put anger into the Throw Away box. It is our choice to obey or to disobey. Cain made a poor choice.

Help With a Heavy Load

Many of the items I had stuffed into the Throw Away box were pretty heavy. In fact, I have known people who weren't able to sort through all the throw-away stuff by themselves. The process was too difficult and they needed help.

In contrast to the counselor who encouraged Mary to confront anyone and everyone and "tell them what you think," there are professionals who adopt a more biblical view. Finding a Christian counselor, psychologist, or member of the clergy to help in the dejunking process is a very viable option. Many times another person can be a big help in identifying clutter for the Throw Away box.

Christian books have also helped me tremendously in the dejunking process, such as *Healing for Damaged Emotions* by David Seamands. Frank Minirth and Paul Meier also have written excellent books, including *Love Is a Choice*. Both of these books helped me with the spring cleaning of my heart because a book can be a wonderful counselor.

Perhaps a friend, Sunday school teacher, or a spouse or other family member can also help you sort through the clutter. I always remind folks that, for a Christian nonprofessional to qualify as a confidant, they must meet two requirements: They must love you and want you to succeed. Unfortunately, not everybody in your life fulfills both. Be discriminating about those with whom you share your clutter.

Speaking of being discriminating, I saw an interesting example of this on a trip I made to visit my dentist. As I parked my car in the small village where he practiced, I noticed that the town marquee had a message that read:

Clean-up Day
Saturday, September 12
Outsiders picking up
Will be arrested.

As I read it I envisioned my dentist's mother visiting from Florida (an obvious "outsider"), picking up a piece of paper in her son's yard, and being arrested. Surely this was not the action the sign was warning against. (Actually, I came to learn that officials were worried that an "unauthorized" scavenger might come to pick up, say, a refrigerator, drop it on his or her foot, and sue the town!)

In the case of our personal "clean-up day"—the dejunking of your heart, mind, and memory—occasionally an outsider is needed to facilitate the process. They will not be arrested.

Reflection

Anger, resentment, and bitterness are potent things that we can be carrying in our clutter. If that is true for you, put them into the Throw Away box.

Maybe the things to throw away are too heavy or the box seems too full already. Find the help you need to continue the dejunking process.

Chapter 6

The Throw Away Rule

Whew! I didn't know if I could fit one more thing into that Throw Away box. Thank goodness it was the biggest. It looked as though I had used every square inch! I was glad that messy job was over, and then I remembered something very important. Mom had a rule about the Throw Away box.

Trash, Not Treasures

The rule was this: Once you throw it away, no digging in the trash! Don't second-guess yourself and take things back out of the box. Those tennis shoes ae too worn out for you to keep and too worn out for you to give away. They are trash, not treasures. Leave them in the Throw Away box.

The guilt you were feeling was bad guilt, not precipitated by any irresponsible or intentional wrongdoing. Leave that guilt in the Throw Away box. That is where it belongs.

You have repented of those sins. Don't drag them back out of the box. They will just clutter up your heart again.

And the hurts you pitched in? You have extended forgiveness

by giving up your "right" to hurt back. Those hurts need to stay in the Throw Away box.

I'm sure you have no desire to pluck back any of the arrogance or selfishness that has been put into the Throw Away box. I was a little embarrassed to find those in my heart in the first place. I certainly don't want to take them back.

The anger you tossed into the box needs to stay there too. Remember Mom's rule: No digging in the trash!

Lessons From Spaghetti

This rule really came home to me one day after my family and I enjoyed a spaghetti dinner. My menu for the evening included spaghetti, garlic bread, and tossed salad. As I finished cooking and set the table, I went to the refrigerator to gather the salad dressing.

Unfortunately, it came as no surprise to me that I had multiple bottles of ranch (fondly referred to in our home as white dressing) and multiple bottles of western (affectionately called red dressing). Does that phenomenon ever occur in your home and refrigerator? Since we know that salad dressing bottles cannot multiply without help, I had always taken full responsibility for the lack of organization (and the abundance of red and white dressing bottles) in my refrigerator door.

Then one day I noticed my son coming from the pantry opening a new bottle of white salad dressing even though there were two of them chilling. I guess that he simply found a fresh bottle more appealing. Or perhaps it is similar to the situation we have experienced many times in our home when any of the males look for something.

"Where is my University of Illinois T-shirt?" asked my half-dressed teenage son.

"It is in your second drawer on the left-hand side," I replied patiently.

"I looked there," he said. "I know it's not in that drawer."

"I'm sure it is," I said confidently. "I just put it in there yesterday."

"Honestly, Mom, I looked," he said desperately. "It's not in the second drawer on the left-hand side."

So I left my easy chair and traipsed upstairs only to find the T-shirt in the second drawer on the left-hand side.

"Son," (you may accurately replace "son" with the name of any of my three boys) I bellowed, "please come upstairs."

Upon his arrival, I opened the second drawer on the left-hand side, picked up the top shirt, and revealed the sought-after University of Illinois T-shirt.

"Here it is," I told him smugly, "in the second drawer on the left-hand side just like I said."

"You didn't say I'd have to look under something," came his reply. And with that he felt completely vindicated.

It has happened countless times. And that is probably what happened with the salad dressing. He somehow couldn't see the multiple bottles in the refrigerator door so it was only logical for him to open a new bottle.

On this particular day, as I prepared to put the dressing on the table, I encountered three red and four white bottles! This, I surmised, was ridiculous. All of the bottles were only partially full, so I decided to consolidate. I poured all the red dressing into one bottle. And I almost accomplished the same task with the white dressing. I was to discover, however, that I had more than one bottle's worth of white dressing.

After the first bottle was filled, I simply took the remaining white dressing and poured it into a bowl. We would use that at dinner. All of the empty bottles of dressing went into the trash and I felt very good about my steps toward organization.

The meal was delicious and when the family was finished eating, each boy took his plate and salad bowl from the table and scraped the remaining contents into the trash. Then they were able to rinse and load the dishwasher. In the meantime, I cleaned off the serving dishes. As I did, I noted that there was still a substantial amount of white dressing in the bowl. No problem, I thought. I had merely misjudged the amount of dressing. I needed to keep two bottles for the white dressing instead of one.

The second bottle was right there in the trash. Oh, wait a minute. Those empty salad dressing bottles were no longer lying on the top of the garbage bag. They were now lying under globs of pasta and spaghetti sauce. They had little carrot pieces sticking to their sides and cucumber seeds dotting their labels. There were crumbs of garlic bread adhered to the open lids and the scene was generally revolting.

As I contemplated reaching into the trash to retrieve an empty salad dressing bottle, I reconsidered. It was not worth it. Mother's rule came alive and I had a new understanding of no digging in the trash. Resist the temptation to dig in your Throw Away box. Leave those things where they belong!

Reflection

You have probably pitched a few things into your own Throw Away box as you have read this book. Were you tempted to fish around in the mess for any of them? If you already managed to retrieve a couple of the thrown-away items, remember Mom's rule and put them back in.

Chapter 7

Let's Give Away Experiences

I turned next to the medium-sized box, the Give Away box. Did I have anything inside of me—in my heart, my mind, or my memory—that I could give away? Did I have anything someone else would want?

As I poked through the clutter, I discovered I had experiences that I could put in the Give Away box. I had gained a certain degree of wisdom from my experiences and all of these were available for the box. I realized also that giving away experience was a very delicate issue: even though the experience might be helpful and wise, it had to be requested to be appreciated. As I thought about it, I remembered just such an occasion several years before, when the recounting of my experiences was actually requested.

Sharing a Day, Sharing Your Lives

Our church family had grown to know and love LeeAnn, a musical evangelist who traveled around the nation and overseas, singing and proclaiming the truth of the gospel. She had scheduled a concert for our congregation, and prior to her visit she phoned our home.

"Hi, Kendra, this is LeeAnn," she announced. "I was wondering what you were doing on Thursday. I have the day free before the concert that evening and would love to spend that time with you."

"What a great idea!" I replied. "I have two speaking engagements in a town about seventy miles away. They'll only take an hour each. We can ride over together, have a great lunch, and maybe you can read a good book or something while I do my speaking."

"Sounds good to me," said LeeAnn, and the deal was closed.

Early Thursday morning we set out together. The travel time was great fun, nonstop talking and laughing and sharing. LeeAnn, at least ten years my junior, had questions about stages and phases of life I had already accomplished that she was yet to tackle. I shared my experiences with her and any God-given wisdom that had been gleaned from those experiences.

The day was delightful and by late afternoon we were back home and I had delivered LeeAnn to the church to prepare for the evening concert. Within a few hours, I was seated in my pew in the church with my family and the concert was ready to begin.

"I had such a wonderful day today," LeeAnn began wistfully. Inwardly I shared her obviously warm feeling and her enthusiasm for the day. "I spent the day," she continued, "with an older Christian woman."

Her statement caught me off guard. Where had she gone after I dropped her off at church? Who was she with next? Then it dawned on me. I was the older Christian woman. It was startling but accurate.

God's Word instructs us as Christian women to invest our time and talents, our experiences and wisdom, in the training of the younger women: "Then they [the older women] can train the younger women …" (Ti 2:4a). We are to put specific experiences and wisdom into the Give Away box that can benefit others. Experiences are very good things to have available in that box. They can help us to "train" those younger than us.

Experience Teaches Us to Respond

Anne was the director of a high-powered group of women. She was a hard-working leader who did her job well and encouraged those around her to do likewise. As a teenager she had been in the youth group my husband and I led, and we had maintained a relationship through the years.

It was not unusual when she called one afternoon to ask my advice on a particular issue at work. "I am really frustrated with one of my top performers," she began. "Marla took it upon herself to consolidate two assignments she was working on and to alter the projected date of completion. I haven't said a word to her yet but I am questioning her judgment in the issue. Have you got time for me to give you some of the details and to bounce things around with me?"

I did have time and Anne spent the next few minutes educating me on some of the specifics of the projects. She didn't expect me to be an expert on the issues in the industry; instead she wondered if I had any wisdom on how to deal with Marla in a Christlike manner.

"I know that your goal is to avoid micromanaging those who report to you," I said. "You will have to evaluate the intelligence of Marla's consolidation of the projects. I do know that you truly respect Marla's technical skill and enthusiasm for the job. I think it is very important how you respond to her. You already made a good decision not to react immediately to the change. I have learned that I can benefit a great deal in my interactions with others if I remember to ask myself the question, What is my goal?

"In this situation, your goal is to honestly evaluate the change and see if it is feasible and then discuss your views in a positive and encouraging way with Marla. You have told me before that your goal is to behave in all aspects of your life in a manner pleasing to God. Your goal is not to take charge and demand that Marla do nothing innovative without first receiving your OK. And your goal is not to embarrass or demean her."

Where did I learn that? From experience! In the old days people used to talk about counting to ten (especially when they experienced anger). I call it choosing to respond rather than react. When you define your goal, it is much easier to respond.

Mother to Mother

The new mother inquired of the well-seasoned mother of six if she could ask her a very important question.

"You are such a great mother," said the new mom. "All six of your children are upstanding citizens. They have all accepted Christ. They are all leaders in their churches and communities. My question is a simple one: Where did you learn to be such a great mom?"

"That, my dear, is an easy question to answer," the older woman replied. "The answer is as simple as two words: good choices."

The new mom seemed a little baffled and was not satisfied with that answer. "May I ask you a second question?" she inquired.

"Absolutely!"

"How did you make those good choices?"

"Elementary. The answer is one simple word: experience."

Still not completely satisfied with the answers she was receiving, the inexperienced mom tried one more time. "I see, and would you be able to tell me where you got all that experience?" she asked, hoping to finally get to the bottom of things.

"Absolutely," the seasoned mom replied. "Bad choices!"

Many times we gain wisdom and experience from what I like to refer to as life lessons. Those are times when I learn from my mistakes. Experience, even experience gained from bad choices, is good for the Give Away box.

A Hair-Raising Experience

It was Wednesday night and the high school Bible study was meeting at our home. Approximately twenty teenagers from several different churches were gathered for the hour of study and the popcorn and cookies to follow.

As the study was wrapping up, I jotted down prayer concerns. After several other kids had shared, Bob asked for prayer for the school play that was to open in about two weeks. I found that a very interesting concern in light of what my two older sons had told me when they arrived home after school that day.

Both Matthew and Aaron had parts in the play. So did Bob. When they had tried out for the parts months before, the director had asked Bob if he would consider cutting his hair for the performance. His hair was not atrociously long, but the part he wanted called for a clean-cut law enforcement officer. Bob told the director that cutting his hair would be no problem and he got the part. Now, weeks later, the director told him that the time had arrived for the haircut and he balked. In fact, he told her he would not get a haircut.

In response to his stance, the director reluctantly gave Bob's part to another actor and relieved Bob of his duties. My boys were not happy. The substitute (who really didn't want the part anyway) now had an extremely short amount of time to memorize a great number of lines.

After all the requests were collected, I prayed and we closed the evening. Then it was time for treats and conversation. Bob joined me in the kitchen and asked if I had heard the news about the change in the cast. I indicated that I had and he went on to tell me his views.

"I don't think it is fair of the director to make me cut my hair," he complained. "There's nothing wrong with the length of my hair. What do you think?"

"Actually, I don't think that this has to do with the length of your hair," I replied. "I think it is a question of integrity."

"Integrity?" Bob questioned. "What do you mean by that?"

"Well, I understand that you and the director had made an agreement during tryouts for the play. You agreed that, when it came time for the performances, you would get a haircut that the director deemed appropriate," I recounted. "So if you now refuse to get that haircut you are going back on your word. It isn't a question of whether or not it is fair for your director to demand a haircut. It is a question of whether or not you will keep your word. It's all about your integrity. And it is my experience that one's integrity is much more important than one's hair."

This definitely gave Bob some food for thought. He left the kitchen and joined some kids in the family room. Before long he returned to my side.

"Guess what I just did, Kendra," he said smiling. "I telephoned my mom and asked her to schedule me for a haircut tomorrow."

"I think that is an excellent decision," I replied. "You have to remember, however, that you might not get your part in the play again. After all, you refused to get a haircut when the director first asked. But I think that what you are doing is the right thing. Who knows what will happen?"

Bob did get a haircut the next day. And the director reconsidered and gave him back his part (much to the delight of everyone on the cast, including Bob's shaking understudy). Bob had gained experience by taking my experience from the Give Away box.

Don't Force It

What if I had forced him to listen to my experience? What if it had been unsolicited? The chances are that my unwanted advice would have landed on deaf ears. When experiences are requested from the Give Away box, they are appreciated.

Items placed in the Give Away box should not be forced upon someone else. As a child, my size 6X party dress was a wonderful thing to give away when I reached size 7, but not every young girl wanted it or could use it. It's better to let folks ask you for the items in the Give Away box or at least suggest an interest in them. Do not force-feed people with your experiences.

As a storyteller by heart and profession, I am often enamored with an experience and feel compelled to share it, even when it has not been requested. Years ago I read that if you were interrupted in the middle of a story and after the interruption no one asked you to complete it, it was an indication that no one really wanted to hear the story in the first place.

I considered that an interesting thought and put it to the test. Before long I was interrupted in the middle of what I considered a very amusing experience. After the brief interlude I waited patiently for someone to ask me to finish my delightful story. When that didn't happen, I had to exercise superhuman control not to go ahead and finish it anyway. The whole incident hurt my feelings. I was so sure that I was giving away a great experience. The next time it happened, I didn't take it so hard. I was learning. Giving away an experience that no one wants is not constructive.

Consider the story in the Gospel of John of the man born blind.

The Jews still did not believe that he [the blind man] had been blind and had received his sight until they sent for the man's parents. "Is this your son?" they asked. "Is this the one you say was born blind? How is it that now he can see?"

"We know he is our son," the parents answered, "and we know he was born blind. But how he can see now, or who opened his eyes, we don't know. Ask him. He is of age; he will speak for himself."

... A second time they summoned the man who had been blind. "Give glory to God," they said. "We know this man [Jesus] is a sinner."

He replied, "Whether he is a sinner or not, I don't know. One thing I do know. I was blind but now I see!"

JOHN 9:18-21, 24

The blind man gave away his experience with Jesus.

Reflection

What experiences have you had (positive or negative) from which you have gained wisdom?

Think of a wonderful experience that taught you a lesson. Jot down that experience. Think of a painful experience that taught you a lesson. Jot that down as well.

Look for opportunities to give away your experiences, but only as they are requested.

Chapter 8

Let's Give Away Memories

Was there anything else that I had accumulated inside of my heart, mind, or memory that I could give away? Was there anything else in my clutter that someone might want? I had an idea. What about putting memories in the Give Away box?

"Tell Me the Story of When ..."

In 1990 something unusual happened to our family. At that time my husband was a KC 135 pilot in the United States Air Force Reserves. He flew a tanker, a plane that refuels military jets. One day in August 1990, Iraq invaded the country of Kuwait. Prior to that day I had never heard of Kuwait and consequently never imagined that this country could have an impact on our lives in central Illinois. As the history books tell us, Kuwait was overrun and many United States forces were called into action.

Within days of the invasion, John was headed for the Middle East. Our boys were all in grade school—kindergarten, fourth grade, and sixth grade—and the idea of their dad being gone to a potential war was not only novel but also a little frightening. They had different reactions and responses to their dad's absence, but I remember distinctly when our oldest son asked me to share a memory with him. He wanted me to put it in the Give Away box. It was a memory that actually belonged to his dad.

"Mom," Matthew said late one evening as the two of us prepared to end the day. "Could you please tell me the story of when Dad was little and was riding his horse, Trigger, and Trigger ran Dad into the barbed wire fence and how Dad got his leg caught on the fence and ripped a big hole in his thigh and how he still has a scar there today? Could you please tell me that story, Mom?"

Now you must realize that the story he just requested was precisely the one he had just recounted. There were no more facts and no more details. That was it! It was the story of Dad's famous riding wound. He obviously knew the story. What was Matthew actually saying? Perhaps it was, "Mom, I miss Dad! If you tell me a story that he has told me many times before, if you'll share that memory with me again, I won't miss him so much."

I heard his question *and* what he was actually saying, so I told the story. I repeated the memory about the time when Dad was little and was riding his horse, Trigger, and Trigger ran Dad into the barbed wire fence and....

And Matthew felt better. Memories are wonderful things we can give away. That evening my eldest son and I went on to create a new memory together. I discovered the comforting power of memories given away, and his response to my sharing of his dad's memory created one I'll always treasure.

I finished the horse story and Matthew sat quietly for just a moment. The words he spoke next touched my heart. "Mom," he began, "you don't have a whole lot of great memories, do you?" He came to that conclusion knowing that I had been raised in the home of an alcoholic and surmising that some of my childhood memories were not positive.

"Oh," I replied, perhaps a little defensively, "I have quite a few good ones."

"Well," he continued, "I'm just glad that when I'm a grown-up and my twelve-year-old asks me about when I was a kid, I'll have lots of good memories to tell him!"

Was I blessed by that reflection from *my* twelve-year-old? You better believe it! I'm thankful that I have that memory to share. *Focus on the Family Bulletin* expresses it well:

> Our kids are shaped forever by the love and training received at home. They will always be influenced by the experiences that characterized the family in which they were raised. No experience is ever completely lost. Even at 50 years of age, they will remember and be guided by that which was taught in childhood. It's an awesome thought. (October 1998)

The Fat Fairy

Among the good memories in our home is the Fat Fairy. She is a combination of Santa Claus, the tooth fairy, the Easter bunny, and every other mythical good guy to hit the planet. She does not take herself too seriously, as evidenced by her unflattering name, but she does supply quarters for missing teeth, poems during Advent, and at least one wrapped gift under the Christmas tree. Who is she? She is Mom, creating memories. (Everyone knows who it is, they just humor me.)

Doughnuts, Doughnuts, Doughnuts

You can choose to create a memory for your family. We did just that during the season of Advent when our older boys were ages five and three. That was the first year that we made doughnuts. It was the first year that we decided to create a memory, a tradition, of sharing a gift of time and taste with our friends at Christmas.

The first few years were experiments in family cooking. We had no idea of the time (or the space) it would take to fix the *Better Homes and Gardens* yeast doughnut recipe times ten! We also had no clue that this exciting adventure that the boys were eagerly awaiting would become boring so quickly. As the doughnuts took shape, thanks to the diligent work of Dad the Doughnut Cutter, we ran into a dilemma. Where do you put all these little masterpieces while they rise?

The dining room table was our first and most logical solution, and we soon discovered it held about ten dozen doughnuts. Unfortunately, we were making twenty dozen! From the dining room table we moved to the dining room floor. As we spread out sheets of waxed paper, I wondered how the doughnuts would ever rise on our drafty floor and what we would do if someone surprised us with a morning visit. Our home at the time was a modest bungalow thirty feet by thirty feet. So the dining room table almost completely filled the space in the dining room; the other ten dozen doughnuts on their waxed paper perches overflowed into the living room and down the hallway. As I look back on the scene, I can see parallels between our early doughnut years and the film *The Blob*. Our doughnuts were overtaking us.

Nevertheless, we finished the task. The doughnuts rose (finally) and we fried them, frosted them, and filled up eight large trays. Then each one of us chose two households to be the recipients of our culinary gift. We wrapped the trays in cellophane, tied each with a ribbon, and were off on our delivery route. We stopped only momentarily at each home on our list. The tray was carried to the door by the one who had selected the stop.

The first year of our doughnut adventure was not an easy one, but it was actually not the most challenging. Imagine the same scene I just described to you (wall-to-wall doughnuts rising at their leisure) and add a crawling baby. Our tradition began before Jonathan's birth and continued even when he was no help at all.

The challenges didn't dissuade us. We continued making the memory. After seven years of doughnut making in our little house, we moved back out to the farm and into a much larger home. The process evolved over the years and so did our kids. I'm not sure if the boys stay enthralled for any longer amounts of time these days than they did in their preschool days, but we certainly do not have to deal with a crawling baby now. And the dining room table is much larger and now holds the same recipe times fourteen. Our quantity has grown proportionately to our taste testers' appetites.

The creation of the memory was intentional and it is one we still enjoy today. Perhaps someday the boys will give away that memory or one like it to their own families.

Memories Are Made of This

Not every memory we have created for our family has been picture perfect. Our kids have memories of many things we have had to apologize for through the years. This is OK too. In addition, unpleasant memories can be healed and mended. If you discover a bad memory inside of you, then put that one in the Give Away box marked "Just for Jesus"; those same memories can eventually help others.

> To preserve this [our rich family heritage] for our children we must tell them where we've been and how we got to this moment. Talking about faith, about early family experiences, about obstacles overcome, or about failures suffered can bring a family together and give it a sense of identity. (*Focus on the Family Bulletin,* April 1998)

I like to combine the elements of a scrapbook and a journal into our family photo albums. For graduation I gave (and will give again) albums to our sons. These record their growth and their achievements, their family and their friends. These albums keep track of a rich heritage and keep their memories alive.

When he graduated from high school, Matthew received a very special gift from one of his uncles. My husband's younger brother, Wynn, has among his many talents the ability to create masterpieces on video. Wynn produced a video story of Matthew's life, using pictures we had taken with our movie camera, footage from school, and still photographs. He dubbed in great music and even interviewed several of Matthew's friends and family members. It was a classic.

As I heard on film of the escapades of Matthew and his friends I laughed. Ramon retold the stories of tutoring sessions Matthew led in the eighth grade. Brian told the story of when they first met in kindergarten. T.J. recounted the comedy of the ill-prepared math contest; Nathan, the emotionally charged, high school football half-time; Tricia, the hilarious drive home from the Illinois Christian Teen Convention. And Bryan told of their shared love of music, Jesus, and each other.

Matthew's brothers gave him advice for college and re-minded him of some of the advice he had given them. His grandparents shared memories. I laughed and I cried, especially when John told of praying for Matthew since his conception, that he would accept Jesus Christ as his Savior. Memories are a wonderful gift to put into the Give Away box.

Walls of Memories

When we walk up to the second story of our home we are greeted with walls of memories. In the fall of 1978, our first child was born. That Christmas, I gave John a large frame filled with a collage of pictures of our newborn child. At the bottom of one snapshot I inserted a slip of paper that read "Merry Christmas, 1978."

The gift was so well received that I repeated it in 1979, 1980, and 1981. That was the year that Aaron was born and joined Matthew in the pictorial trip down memory lane. I made another one in 1982, 1983, 1984, and 1985. That year we were the proud parents of "My Three Sons" as Jonathan was added to the family.

The tradition has continued. Those frames record memories of the boys' athletic adventures, musical conquests, and assorted pets. There are pictures of our family vacations and of special friends and extended family who have touched our lives through the years. There are pictures, for example, of our eight-day Canadian wilderness canoe trip. That was the trip we took instead of buying carpeting. I'm a little ashamed that I even had the debate—carpet versus Canada. Thank goodness Canada and its memories won the contest.

Memories ... right there on the wall. The frames wind around the hallway of the open staircase in chronological order, beginning near our bedroom door. On more than one occasion, I have spotted John standing and studying this history in pictures, this record of our family memories.

"Have twenty years really gone by already? My, how the boys have grown." It reminds me of how Jesus' growth was journaled too, in Luke 2:52: "And Jesus grew in wisdom and stature, and in favor with God and men."

Staking Their Claim

My husband and I have worked with the youth of our church for over fifteen years. One of our goals has always been to help them remember the things God has done in their lives—to keep those memories alive. Many have come to a saving knowledge of Christ in conjunction with some experience we have had together as a youth group. Many have seen a verse or verses from God's Word come alive in their lives. When one of our teens realizes and internalizes a truth from God, we encourage them to "Drive a stake behind the barn."

What does that mean? In our rural community, it could literally mean to hammer a stake behind one of the outbuildings on a student's family farm. Or for our town kids it could mean to pound in a stake behind the garage. What is the purpose? We create a concrete illustration to remind them of the reality of their experience with God, just as the psalmist urges: "Remember the wonders he has done, his miracles, and the judgments he pronounced" (Ps 105:5).

The memory of that reality is a treasure for them and for others, for it is a memory they can give away. The stake is there to see. It can be touched and cannot be imagined away. Satan will try to convince folks that their experience with God and the illumination of His Word in their hearts were nothing more than figments of their imagination. That stake behind the barn reminds the believer of the reality of the memory.

Journaling can reap the same benefits. When you write in a journal, you record the event and preserve the memory. Retelling the incident can also retain the memory. God's Word tells us, "That if you confess with your mouth, 'Jesus is Lord,' and believe in your heart that God raised him from the dead, you will be saved" (Rom 10:9). Among other things, confession helps to confirm the reality of the event of our salvation. It keeps it alive in our memory.

David prayed, "Restore to me the joy of your salvation" (Ps 51:12). The joy of Christ's salvation and of hearing personally from God's Word can be restored and rekindled by reading the account again in your journal, by retelling your memory, or by glancing at the stake behind the barn.

"He [God] has caused his wonders to be remembered; the Lord is gracious and compassionate" (Ps 111:4).

Reflection

What is one of your favorite childhood memories? What other warm memories do you have that could bring comfort to another?

Jot down a memory of when God's Word spoke directly to you. Have you "driven a stake behind the barn"? Writing down the memory on this page will help to preserve it.

Who might benefit from hearing the memory you have of the Word of God coming alive to you? Look for a God-supplied opportunity to share that memory with someone.

Chapter 9

Let's Give Away Encouragement

As a young girl cleaning my room, I often tried to reason that, if I had the job half done, it was more finished than it was when I started. So maybe I didn't have to actually finish the entire dejunking process. Trust me, that logic got me nowhere.

God encouraged me to finish the job of dejunking my heart by looking for other things to give away to others. In fact, encouragement was one of them.

Encouraged to Be Encouragers

Paul's first letter to the Thessalonians encourages us to be encouragers: "Therefore encourage one another and build each other up, just as in fact you are doing"(5:11). Note also what this verse does *not* say. We do not read, "Therefore discourage one another and tear each other down just as in fact you are doing." I have occasionally seen, however, discouragement being put into the Give Away box, even by members of the family of God. The world does enough to discourage people; we don't need to help.

"Do not let any unwholesome talk come out of your mouths, but only what is helpful for building others up according to their needs, that it may benefit those who listen" (Eph 4:29). When was the last time you or any adult in your family was applauded at work? Too often the workplace is permeated with a negative atmosphere instead of a positive one.

When was the last time your child came home from school elated over some encouragement he or she had received? When was the last time he came home discouraged and deflated? My guess is that the latter happens more frequently. When we started a family, I chose to be an at-home mom. There were times I was discouraged in my own home. In fact, I can still remember my husband announcing one day that he had figured out why being a homemaker was so tough. He went on to explain that a significant portion of my "job" in the home was to see that everything ran smoothly. Of course, when everyone's life was running smoothly, no one noticed. But let me get behind with the wash or let the meals become boring and repetitive, and someone was quick to comment.

"Peanut butter and jelly again?"

"Where is my baseball uniform? Isn't it washed yet?"

"Golly, Mom, what in the world have you been doing?"

"Being a homemaker is tough," John concluded, "because we only notice when you're not doing it perfectly."

That can be discouraging. It is also discouraging to realize that life is not fair. We want things to be equitable. The truth is, though, that if things cannot be completely fair, we hope the scales of justice will tip in our direction.

Life can be discouraging. This is no surprise to God. There

are situations we encounter that tear us down, but it is important that we remember God's Word and not contribute to the discouragement. We are to encourage one another and build each other up. Psychologist and author Abraham Maslow once said, "It takes nine affirming comments to make up for each critical comment we give our children" (*Focus on the Family Bulletin,* April 1998). In my words, for every kick-in-the-shin you get in life, it takes nine atta-boys to recover. I think that is probably true with adults too.

When I examined my internal clutter, when I started spring cleaning my heart, I recognized that I had encouragement inside of me that I could give away. Everyone needs it, young and old, because everyone lives in a world where folks are kicking at their shins.

The Power of Encouragement

Encouragement is a powerful tool. I saw an amazing example of it one summer when Jonathan played baseball. John was his coach. The league rules stipulated that if your team did not have enough players and the opponents had more than enough, you could borrow a player for the game. This system obviously had some strengths and some weaknesses. It made the teams equal in number. It gave a potential bench-sitter on the overpopulated team an opportunity to start and play the entire game. But it also pulled at the loyalty of the temporarily traded ballplayer.

John's team found itself one player short for the first game of a tournament. John went to the opposing bench, where three boys were "riding the pines."

"Would one of you guys like to play for us tonight?" John asked.

Two of the boys immediately said no. That left Donald. Deep in the recesses of his thirteen-year-old heart, I'm sure he realized that he would now get an entire game of playing time, in contrast to the one inning he was destined for on his own team. At the same time, he realized that he would be a traitor if, miraculously, he performed well.

Donald joined John's team and was put at the end of the batting order. By the second inning, he was at the plate facing his own team's number-one pitcher. As Donald approached the plate, John—by nature, nurture, and choice a great encourager—began to cheer. "You can do it, Donald. You can get a hit," he shouted, clapping his hands. "Stand right in there. You can do it!"

And Donald did do it! He slammed one into the outfield and scurried to first base. Although I certainly did not witness each one of Donald's "at-bats" throughout the season, it is my guess that none of his other hits were as impressive (or brought such accolades). By now the bench of Donald's adopted team was cheering too, joining John in their approval of his great hit.

The excitement was not over yet. Under John's skillful direction and encouragement, Donald stole second. The next batter got a hit and Donald took off for third. "Slide, Donald, slide," shouted John as his body language pulled the runner to third base.

The throw was made but Donald slid under the tag. He was

safe. As he stood up and dusted himself off, Donald smiled from ear to ear. The roar of his temporary teammates and the encouraging applause of his adopted coach and the crowd added to his pleasure and pride.

"That's great, Donald," John said smiling. "I knew you could do it!"

The next batter's hit sent Donald on his way to home plate and he scored for the team. As he returned to the bench John congratulated him.

"You know, Coach," he said, "I've been detasseling corn this summer and I think I got that good hit because my wrists are stronger."

"I'll bet you're right," John said, smiling at the joy this young man was experiencing. Donald, destined to sit the bench for his own team, had temporarily switched loyalties and had scored a run.

Could he have done it without the encouragement? We will never know, will we? I personally don't think he would have even rounded first base.

The Gutter Theory

Encouragement can be such a simple thing. When I was writing my first book, *Empowered by Choice,* I would write until I ran into a brick wall and then I would call my editor.

"You can do it," she would say. "I know you can do it." That was all it took. Her encouragement and confidence gave me confidence.

Some people, however, never seem to be able to encourage another person. They are perpetually negative and seldom complimentary. I have discovered a common denominator among these discouragers: they are discouraged themselves. These people spend a great deal of time and energy kicking other folks in the shins because they hope it will make their bruised shins feel better.

They are perfect illustrations of the Gutter Theory, which states that people who are in the gutter do everything they can to pull others down with them. No one wants to be in the gutter alone. Misery really does love company.

The people living the Gutter Theory, the people with bruised shins themselves, need encouragement just as much, maybe even more, than everyone else does. How sad it is that my natural tendency is to withhold my encouragement from these negative people because I have determined that they don't deserve it. Instead, I need to heed the Word of God and encourage without being selective.

A cartoon on our refrigerator features a little boy who is obviously discouraged.

"What's wrong?" his mother asks.

"No one likes me," the young boy replies.

"That's not true," his mother says encouragingly. "I like you!"

"Of course you do," he counters. "That's your job!"

Isn't that the job for all of us as Christians—not necessarily to *like* everyone, as we would our own children, but to be encouragers? Encouragement is something in the Give Away box that doesn't have to be requested to be appreciated. It can be freely given.

Step-by-Step Encouragement

I remember when our youngest son learned to walk. He had obviously been toying with the idea for several weeks. In fact, I told his older brothers to keep on the lookout for his first steps. I knew it wouldn't be long.

One Sunday after church I went into the kitchen to prepare dinner, and John settled in front of the television to catch a few minutes of football. The boys grabbed some Matchbox cars and joined their dad in the living room for a little road racing before lunch.

Within minutes, Jonathan abandoned his cars and crawled over to the couch. He pulled himself up. Then he glanced around the room as though he were taking roll.

"Mom, you really need to get out here from the kitchen to see this."

"Dad, look over here."

"Matthew, Aaron, are you watching?"

His wordless roll call somehow managed to get everyone's attention. When all eyes were on him, he turned and steadied himself. Then he let go of the couch, took one step, and down he went.

As he looked up from his cushy, diaper-padded seat, the crowd went wild.

"Great job, Jonathan," Matthew shouted. "Give me five, big guy."

"That was super!" Aaron chimed in.

"Hooray for Jonathan," said his father and I as we contributed to the cheering section.

Jonathan was obviously pleased and I imagined him thinking, "Ah, yes. This is everything Gordon said it would be!" (Gordon was his church nursery buddy who was a few months older.)

Jonathan crawled back over to the couch, pulled himself up, and glanced around the room to be sure every eye was on him. He turned, steadied himself, took one step, and then two steps. This was almost too much for his fans.

"Hey, Jonathan," cheered Matthew. "You are the best."

"That was great walking!" encouraged Aaron.

"Yea, Jonathan!" we added.

That was many years ago. Today Jonathan walks, runs, skips, hops, jumps, and dances with his mother at weddings and July 4th celebrations. How did he get so good? He just kept trying and we just kept applauding.

More than once I have wondered what would have happened if the scene had gone like this ...

... His wordless roll call somehow managed to get everyone's attention. When all eyes were on him, he turned and steadied himself. Then he let go of the couch, took one step, and down he went.

As he looked up from his cushy, diaper-padded seat, the crowd responded rather coolly.

"What were you trying to do, Jonathan?" asked Matthew.

"Was that supposed to be walking?" wondered Aaron.

"Yes, Jonathan. What were you doing? You obviously can't walk," I added.

"Please don't try again," said John. "You might hurt yourself."

Jonathan was obviously confused and he thought to himself, "Wait a minute. This isn't what Gordon said would happen. Maybe I did something wrong. I'll try again."

Jonathan crawled back over to the couch, pulled himself up, and glanced around the room to be sure every eye was on him. He turned, steadied himself, took one step, and then two steps.

"Please, Jonathan," said Matthew. "Don't do that again. You are obviously too short to walk."

"Thank goodness he is short," Aaron added. "He keeps falling down!"

"That will be enough of that silliness. You cannot walk, so quit trying," said his father and I to top off the discouragement.

Does that make you angry or disgusted or generally frustrated with everyone except Jonathan? Of course it does! Thankfully, very few people would ever speak to a one-year-old that way. Yet we choose to speak in a disparaging way to folks that are a little older.

"*You* are going to fix the plumbing? You're not calling a professional? I really don't think we can afford to have you fix the plumbing."

"Why did you make a B– in spelling? That is ridiculous! Spelling is just memorization."

We offer discouragement rather than encouragement. "Therefore encourage one another and build each other up"— even in your own home? Perhaps especially in your own home. Encourage that family member who is aspiring to accomplish something new.

The Perfect Name

More than once in the Bible we are introduced to someone who was once called by one name but is now called by another. "Joseph, a Levite from Cyprus, whom the apostles called Barnabas (which means Son of Encouragement), sold a field he owned and brought the money and put it at the apostles' feet" (Acts 4:36-37).

They changed this young man's name to Barnabas, son of encouragement. With a name like that, you can imagine that he had no difficulty being a supporter to those around him.

> News of this [a great number of people turning to the Lord] reached the ears of the church at Jerusalem, and they sent Barnabas to Antioch. When he arrived and saw the evidence of the grace of God, he was glad and encouraged them all to remain true to the Lord with all their hearts.
>
> ACTS 11:22-23

Barnabas gave the believers the best encouragement anyone can give or receive. Encouragement is a good thing for the Give Away box.

Reflection

Can you remember a time when someone's encouragement spurred you on?

When was the last time you gave away encouragement to someone else?

Think of a person you know who could use some encouragement. Make a plan now to put encouragement into the Give Away box.

Chapter 10

Let's Give Away Our Faith

I continued to rummage in my clutter and discovered that I had faith inside of me that would be the perfect addition to the Give Away box. How did I know it would make such a great contribution? Because I had had the privilege and blessing of being the recipient as someone shared his faith and put it into the Give Away box.

A Summertime Meeting

As a young girl I was taught the value and satisfaction of hard work. Growing up in central Illinois provided me with a good job opportunity as young as age thirteen, when I could be employed by one of the seed corn companies to detassel corn. You may remember that Donald, the temporarily traded baseball player, gave detasseling corn the credit for his increased wrist strength and improved batting. Because I know many of you are still scratching your heads in wonder at this, let me explain.

Hybrid seed corn companies want to control the pollination

of corn plants by preventing the plants from self-pollinating—the process of pollen traveling from the tassel on the top of the plant down the silk to the ear. So they hire teenagers to ride on funny-looking machines or to walk through the rows of corn and remove the tassels—hence, detasseling.

The job was hard work, the starting time was ridiculously early, and the conditions (wet, sharp corn leaves in the early morning hours followed by sweltering heat) were undesirable. Why would any teenager want this job? The pay wasn't too bad and it was about the only job available before turning sixteen years old. Then, however, many doors were open for employment. You could, for example, take senior lifesaving and become a lifeguard at the swimming pool.

The summer I was sixteen I carefully weighed the options. The job at the pool was not difficult. The hours were great, with a starting time late enough to encourage the nocturnal habits of teenagers. The conditions were near perfect with beautiful sunshine and plentiful socialization. OK, the pay was poor, but after weighing the pros and cons for a good five minutes, I signed up for senior lifesaving. (Actually it may not have taken the entire five minutes.)

The course was three weeks long. We learned Red Cross lifesaving skills, were instructed in first aid, and worked to increase our swimming stamina. The last three days constituted the final exam. We had a written test, an endurance swim, and, finally, on the last day, we were scheduled to "rescue the victim."

When we arrived at the pool on the last day, I noticed that our instructor was not alone. With him was a very good-looking young man with blond hair and big muscles. It turned out that the visitor was the instructor's younger brother there to help with the test. As I moved toward the younger brother's line, I realized that I was not alone. Every other girl had made the same decision. So I got into his line first. And as I like to say at our house, "Mom got Dad in a cross-chest carry and just never let go!"

That is how I met my husband. We had our first date that afternoon and were married four years later. Most of the dating years were pleasant, but I remember one incident that left me a little uncertain about the possible future of our relationship. When I was a senior in high school, I was having a major catastrophe. It has been my experience that most teenage girls have multiple major catastrophes that they too will forget as adults (or maybe even as older teens). My catastrophe was so serious that I shared it with my boyfriend, John. Although I've forgotten what provoked the crisis, I vividly remember his response. He listened intently to my situation and then drew in a deep breath and suggested that I pray about it.

"Pray about it?" I thought. "What does God have to do with this whole thing? Surely He is too busy with gravity and the galaxy to care about what is bothering me!"

After John left my home that evening I wondered what would become of our romance. Pray about it! I had never heard of anything so ridiculous. Our romance did not disintegrate, however, because I refocused my vision on his finer points. Remember I mentioned he was really cute? I decided that it was OK if he was a little bit different.

The Key Difference

What was different about him? At nineteen years of age, he was a Christian. At age sixteen he had accepted Christ when an evangelist had visited the little church his family attended. John talked to God and listened to Him from that point forward, but he received very little instruction in God's Word. He had no idea that the Bible said not to be unequally yoked: "Do not be yoked together with unbelievers. For what do righteousness and wickedness have in common? Or what fellowship can light have with darkness?" (2 Cor 6:14).

So, four years after we met, he yoked up with me. We were married and one week later we drove to west Texas, where John was in pilot training. He was having a wonderful time learning about jets and anticipating flying them. He was also driving me crazy!

He had a peace about him that was more than I could understand (or stand at all). He absolutely refused to worry about things I felt warranted some concentrated worry. He seemed to pray about everything, even little things like where we would live and where I would work. Worst of all, he exemplified the fruits of the Spirit described in Galations 5—love, joy, peace, patience, kindness, goodness, faithfulness, gentleness, and self-control—almost all the time.

Finally, one evening when we had only been married a few months, I asked John to explain to me why he was having such a good time and I was so obviously miserable. It was just the opening he had been waiting for.

"I think the difference could be that I have accepted Christ as my Savior and I'm not sure you have done that yet," he said gently.

He didn't talk about denominations or their differences. He didn't tell me I was bound for hell (although I think it was a stretch of kindness to say he "wasn't sure I had done that yet"). He simply lived his faith and then shared it. He put it in the Give Away box and I snatched it out.

"That probably is the difference," I replied. "What do we do about it?"

A simple prayer of repentance and faith is what we did about it. John gave away his faith.

Opportunities Abound

There are plenty of opportunities for each one of us to give away our faith. Sometimes the opportunities are structured, planned, calculated, and extensively prayed about. Sometimes they present themselves spontaneously.

When my two older boys were little we often went to the library. It was a fun outing and all three of us looked forward to it. One day, as we laughed and read and picked out our pile of books, the librarian came over to join us.

"You always seem so filled with joy," she said. "What is your secret?"

Wow! What an opening! What a perfect opportunity to share about Christ. So what did I say? "Gee, I don't know," I replied. "I guess I just got enough sleep last night."

Now that is really spiritual. A reply like that is bound to

make a difference for the kingdom of God. I realized almost immediately that I had missed an opportunity. Later in the week I was reading in the Bible in 1 Peter 3:15: "But in your hearts set apart Christ as Lord. Always be prepared to give an answer to everyone who asks you to give the reason for the hope that you have."

It couldn't have been much clearer. I was not prepared to give an account of my hope. After reading that verse I asked God to give me another chance with the librarian. I've learned that many times if we miss the 8:05, God will allow us to take the 9:05. Sure enough, on one of the next few visits, the librarian presented me with a wonderful opening to share my faith. This time I was prepared. Faith is a good thing to put in the Give Away box.

Sharing our faith, putting it into the Give Away box as we spring clean our hearts, can result in different responses from those who receive it. I gladly embraced the faith when my husband put his in the Give Away box. The librarian welcomed my sharing my faith and it seemed to bolster hers.

And Then There Was Joe

Joe had been a friend of our family for years. He was a gruff older man who successfully hid his tender heart from almost everyone who knew him. He couldn't hide it from me, though. He and his wife were very private, but our paths intersected often enough that our family grew to love them. Joe and Beth were unchurched. I don't believe that they ever went to church, not even when they were raising their children. They knew that we went to church each Sunday, yet they didn't seem to be offended by that commitment in our lives.

If they were questioned, my guess is that they would have called us good friends even though the connection between the elderly couple and our family was quite sporadic and infrequent. When Joe and Beth had some financial trouble, we were aware of the circumstances and I prayed for them. When Beth had health problems, I was able to help her out with transportation. And Joe and Beth both found many ways to be a blessing to our three sons through the years.

Whenever we would part after one of our occasional times together I would remind them, "We love you."

Joe and Beth did not return the phrase and I never expected it. I'm sure they found the idea of our family loving theirs a little unusual and slightly uncomfortable. I told this elderly couple that I loved them, but I never told them about Jesus or how much He loved them.

Then one night I had a dream. In my dream, Joe and Beth were driving down the highway in their beat-up car and had a fatal accident. The dream continued and both Joe and Beth, though dead, talked to me.

"Why didn't you tell us?" they asked me in unison. "Why didn't you tell us about Jesus? We are dead and now it is too late!"

I woke from that dream with a start and I could remember all of the details. When morning came I told them to John.

"God spoke to me in that dream," I explained. "I don't think Joe and Beth are on the verge of a fatal car accident.

That's not what God was telling me. He was letting me know that I need to share my faith with them."

God had never spoken to me in a dream before and has not done so since, but there was no doubt in my mind that it was a message from Him. To be honest, though, I was not very excited about the possibility of sharing my faith. My relationship with Joe and Beth was very comfortable. They both liked me and were not threatened by me. I guess in a sense I was a little threatened by them. Many questions buzzed through my mind.

"What if I share my faith and they laugh at me?"

"What if they sever all ties with our family? The boys would miss their kindness."

"What if they become angry with me?"

"What if they belittle me?"

Where did these questions come from? Not from my family and not from God. Perhaps it was my insecurity or my pride or maybe it was the enemy himself. Finally I heard a question in my mind that I was forced to answer.

"You say I am number one in your life. You say you love Joe and Beth. Yet you fail to tell them about me. Which of the two statements is a lie—your love for me or your love for Joe and Beth?" Which statement was a lie? Could I leave Jesus out of my friendship with Joe and Beth if He was truly number one in my life? No, I admitted, I could not. So I began to seek the opening to give away my faith.

Within weeks of the dream and my realization of its significance, I had the chance to take Beth to a nearby community for some shopping. I told her my story of repentance and redemption. I told her my understanding of God's plan of salvation and I told her of my dream. She listened intently and thanked me for sharing these things with her. The conversation continued a few minutes longer and then the topic shifted. I knew that seeds had been planted.

Weeks later I noticed Joe's truck in the parking lot of a local shop where he sometimes worked. He was the only one in the store when I stopped and I asked him for a few minutes of his time. I told Joe of my dream and then I proceeded to do a monologue on salvation and closed with the same tough question God had given me.

"So," I concluded, "I realized that if I say Jesus is number one in my life and I tell you and Beth we love you but fail to tell you about Him, I am a liar."

Joe just stood and stared at me. He didn't seem to be particularly angry or even more than politely interested. Finally I broke the silence.

"Do you understand what I said?" I asked him.

"Yes, I do," he replied. And that was it.

The conversation didn't end as I had hoped or secretly planned. There was no sinner's prayer or repentant attitude. I put my faith in the Give Away box and Joe took a look at it and left it there in the box. Sometimes that happens. It should not, however, dissuade us from giving away our faith. As long as we are the fragrance of Christ (as opposed to a stench) we can feel free to give away our faith.

It is not our job to convince, debate, or coerce. Our job is to live the faith we give away. And that is what I still have the opportunity to do with Joe and Beth. My conversations don't seem to have changed their lives yet, but they didn't break our ties of friendship either. I can now be sure they have heard the gospel message. Now they can make the choice to respond. When we put our faith into the Give Away box we oftentimes do not know when or if another will take it out.

Timing Can Be Crucial

One letter I wrote to a friend was the equivalent of putting my faith in the Give Away box. I had typed it, single-spaced, and made a carbon copy for my files, which I still have. (That format should let you know how long ago it was written.) The friend was about twelve years my senior and was going through a difficult time in her life.

I do not remember her precise words in response to my letter, but I do remember the tone of her reply. It was very condescending and patronizing. It was as though she was saying (as she patted me on the head), "That's nice that this religion stuff works for you, Kendra. But someday you'll grow out of it." She did not take my faith out of the Give Away box. But she did not destroy it either. Instead, that faith (and the original copy of my letter) just stayed put for awhile. My faith rested in the Give Away box. My letter rested in her jewelry box.

Eight years later a crisis hit her life. She was extremely ill—so sick that the doctors gave her no chance for recovery. On a visit to her bedside, I found the perfect opportunity to replay the contents of my letter, an opportune moment to present the gospel again.

This time her response was quite different. My friend did not demean my faith. Instead she adopted it as she prayed to receive Jesus as her Savior. Days later her time on earth was over. We never know when the faith we put into the Give Away box will be received.

A teenage boy I know shared his faith with one of his teammates one night after practice.

"I know you are probably right about this Jesus stuff," was the response, "but I'm just not ready for it yet."

When would he be ready? Would he someday, maybe eight years later, find himself face to face with a deadly disease and then proclaim himself ready?

No, this young man didn't have that opportunity (if I can label a serious disease an opportunity). Instead, a few weeks later, his life and his older brother's ended in an auto accident. The ballplayer who had shared his faith was devastated. Why hadn't his friend accepted Christ when they talked? Why hadn't he made that choice before it was too late?

In an effort to comfort my young friend after the sudden death of his teammate, it dawned on me once again that we never know when or if someone retrieves the faith we have put into the Give Away box. "While we are on earth we will not know what transpired during your friend's last seconds on earth," I began. "It is possible that in that brief time between the realization of the impending accident and the impact itself, your friend might have spoken the name of Jesus in faith … believing that He was the Son of God and his Savior."

We don't know if that happened. We don't know if in the last second of his life this teenage boy reached into the Give

Away box and snatched out faith in God for his own. We do know, however, that there was faith in the Give Away box. His friend and teammate had put it in there for him to grasp. Giving away your faith can make an impression that you might never know on earth.

No Assumptions

Our youth group was preparing to present a sunrise worship service for the church. That year the kids had decided that, instead of an outside speaker, one of the group would present the morning message.

When Gene volunteered for the job I was very pleased. He was a great kid and a leader in our group. And he was, I thought, a Christian. After he volunteered for the preaching assignment and the other teens had accepted other positions, I told all of them that I would be available to help them in any way I could.

Days later, Gene asked me if I could listen to the message he was preparing. We met at the church and Gene read me his sermon. It was very sterile and actually quite boring. I listened attentively and racked my brain deciding how I would tell him that this message had very little meaning.

"Well," I began when he concluded his presentation, "I had an idea while you were reading your message. It would be a little different slant than what you've taken, but I think it might be very meaningful. What if you simply told the congregation about your experience when you accepted Christ as your

Savior? People's personal testimonies can be very powerful."

Gene just looked at me in a pleading manner. It was then that I realized that this terrific kid, this super role model, this great leader, had never accepted Christ as his Savior.

"Have you asked Christ into your heart yet?" I asked very gently and matter-of-factly. "Would you like to do it now?"

Gene's pleading expression turned to one of relief as he enthusiastically nodded yes. We prayed together right there on the floor of the lecture room.

At the sunrise service on Sunday, Gene presented the message. It was meaningful and powerful. It was about his personal commitment to Jesus Christ that had happened just days before. Not only did we hear the gospel message that Sunday morning, I also heard the message that I should never let a presumption keep me from giving away my faith. Because Gene was churched and had heard the gospel more than once, because he was a great kid, I had assumed that he had a personal relationship with Jesus. Never let an assumption block you from putting your faith in the Give Away box, making it available to another.

Drawing Faith as Well as Water

The woman at the well had a noontime encounter with Jesus at a well near the town of Sychar (see John 4:1-42). She had gone to draw water from the well, but she had waited until later in the day when the town meeting place would be desolate.

She was startled to see Jesus at the well and surprised when He addressed her. After all, she was a woman—and a Samaritan woman besides, and Jews did not associate with Samaritans. When Jesus asked her for a drink and then told her about the living water He made available, the woman was puzzled.

"Sir," the woman said, "you have nothing to draw with and the well is deep. Where can you get this living water? Are you greater than our father Jacob, who gave us the well and drank from it himself, as did also his sons and his flocks and herds?"

Jesus answered, "Everyone who drinks this water will be thirsty again, but whoever drinks the water I give him will never thirst. Indeed, the water I give him will become in him a spring of water welling up to eternal life."

The woman said to him, "Sir, give me this water so that I won't get thirsty and have to keep coming here to draw water."

He told her, "Go, call your husband and come back."

"I have no husband," she replied.

Jesus said to her, "You are right when you say you have no husband. The fact is, you have had five husbands, and the man you now have is not your husband. What you have just said is quite true."

"Sir," the woman said, "I can see that you are a prophet."

JOHN 4:11-19

The woman at the well had gone from puzzled to amazed. This stranger knew all about her. When she realized this, she put down her water jar and ran back to town to tell the others.

"Come, see a man who told me everything I ever did. Could this be the Christ?" (4:29). And the people did come. She put her faith into the Give Away box. She shared it with others in the town, perhaps even with those she had been avoiding by arriving at the well so late in the day.

> Many of the Samaritans from that town believed in him [Jesus] because of the woman's testimony, "He told me everything I ever did." So when the Samaritans came to him, they urged him to stay with them, and he stayed two days. And because of his words many more became believers.
> They said to the woman, "We no longer believe just because of what you said; now we have heard for ourselves, and we know that this man really is the Savior of the world."
>
> JOHN 4:39-42

The Samaritan woman put her faith into the Give Away box and her neighbors took it out. First they believed just because of what the woman said. Then they believed because they had personally identified and accepted Christ as the Savior of the world. Now they also had faith to give away.

Reflection

Have you accepted Christ as your Savior? Did it happen as a result of someone else putting his or her faith in the Give Away box?

Have you ever articulated your salvation story? Take a minute to recall the story of the birth of your faith. Jot down an outline of that experience here. Who? What? Where? When? How?

Now that you can put your acceptance of Christ into words, you are prepared to share about the hope that is within you. God will provide an opportunity.

If you have not been born again, there is no time like the present. Know that:

- God is holy and perfect; we are sinners and cannot save ourselves (see 1 Peter 1:16; Revelation 4:11; Romans 3:23; Isaiah 59:2).
- God provided Jesus Christ to be the perfect substitute to die in our place (see Romans 5:8; John 14:6).
- Our response must be to receive Jesus Christ by faith as Savior and Lord (see John 1:12-13; 5:24). You can do this by simply praying ...

> "Lord Jesus, I need you. I realize I'm a sinner and I can't save myself. I need your mercy. I believe that you died on the cross for my sins and rose from the dead. I repent of my sins and put my faith in you as Savior and Lord. Take control of my life and help me to follow you in obedience. In Jesus' name, Amen."

> *More Than Winning: Discovering God's Plan for Your Life*
> (Fellowship of Christian Athletes, 1986)

Then respond to Jesus in a life of obedience (see Luke 9:23).

Chapter 11

Let's Give Away Prayer

The Give Away box was about as full as it could get. Still, as I continued the spring cleaning of my heart, I found at least one more thing for it. I could give away prayer.

God's Word talks a lot about prayer—things about it that I understand and many things about it that baffle me. The whole idea that the creator of the universe is ready, willing, and able to talk with me is mind-boggling. More than that, He actually desires that communication.

Our oldest son is in college. Although the campus is only fifty miles away from home, I miss him. I don't miss his dirty laundry (probably because he does a good job of accumulating it for his trips home). I don't miss the empty gas tank on my van. More than anything I miss talking to him; many times in his high school years he kept his father and me up later than usual to discuss something important. When he went to college, I tried very hard to do two things: to be available and not distracted when he called and to not bug him with a call just because I was lonely.

It is fun to talk with Matthew. It is even better to talk with God. With God I also want to be available and not distracted when I hear His voice, but, in contrast to my teenage son, my calls never bug Him. He is glad to hear from me when I am lonely or happy or sad or afraid.

And we don't have to wait in line for God or experience the frustration of call-waiting. He is never too busy. He is never disinterested. He is available, attentive, and able. He is caring, compassionate, and communicative, desiring communication with us.

The Habit of Prayer

Praying with and for your family is a wonderful thing to give away. Almost every morning during the school year our family eats breakfast together and we finish the meal with prayer. As the boys grow up and leave our home, they know the routine. They know that we will be praying for them and their needs at the start of each day.

For almost fourteen years John and I have fasted on Wednesday. On that day we pray for each one of our boys and for one another. Many times there are other concerns that we also lift to God during the day. Although Wednesday is not our only day of prayer, we have set aside that specific day each week to give away prayer.

The first time I read the Bible verse "pray without ceasing" (1 Thes 5:17, KJV), I was puzzled by it. How could I pray constantly? Wouldn't bowing my head and closing my eyes be a dangerous posture on the highway? Yes, it certainly would and this verse has nothing to do with the posture of my body. It has everything to do with the posture of my heart.

To pray without ceasing means to have a constant God-consciousness, to have an awareness of God Almighty regardless of my location or preoccupation at the time. It would seem that God calls us to put prayer into the Give Away box all the time.

My prayers are not fancy. I remember hearing a woman speak on prayer. Although she was very articulate and talked about such appropriate points as the availability of God, her flowery vocabulary momentarily made me feel that God was beyond the range of my regular voice with its regular tone and regular words. But the feeling was only temporary. I soon remembered that I did not have to learn a whole new vocabulary or pronounce the word *God* as though it had two syllables in order to communicate with my Savior. I could talk to Him as a child talks to his or her daddy.

Or, as a friend told my husband one day after Sunday school, "When you pray you talk to God like He is your friend." God is our friend, a friend who relishes our prayers. He wants us to talk to Him. Do you avail yourself of this? God's Word says we can "approach the throne of grace with confidence" (Heb 4:16). We are welcomed and encouraged to converse with God.

Broken In

John and I have owned one new car in our lives. We bought a van several years ago that had only five miles on the odometer when we drove it off the lot. New vans have family rules that old vans don't have, such as: No eating in the van until it is broken in.

After we had owned the van for one week, I loaded it up with gas and with two girlfriends and headed to a Christian conference. We enjoyed three great days of laughing and learning and were finally heading home. The drive was filled with even more laughter and talk as we cruised down a two-lane highway in Indiana.

Suddenly a car, which had come to a stop at a crossroad just ahead of the van, pulled out to cross the highway. Immediately I saw what was happening and put my brakes on hard. The new van skidded and swerved and rocks flew as the back tires went onto the shoulder.

As we realized that a collision was imminent, all three of us began to pray out loud.

"Jesus, help us. Protect us."

"Protect the driver of the other car."

"Be with us, Lord."

In the next moment there was a loud crash and the van and the other car collided. As both vehicles came to an abrupt halt, all three of us continued to pray for the woman in the car that had pulled out in front of us. Fortunately, the van just grazed the back left bumper of the car, seemingly doing little damage to the car or the driver. Our prayers for her safety and ours had been answered.

The van had almost missed the car. The key word is *almost*. We did minimal damage to the car; however, the van was another story. It looked as though a very large car-eating animal (a car-nivore, no doubt) had taken a huge bite out of it. One headlight was hanging by a wire. The grillwork had disintegrated. And there were car parts showing that definitely had no business showing.

I went to the police station to call home. "John, I've had an accident," I reported, "but we are all OK, thanks to God."

"How is the van?" he asked. "Can you drive it home?"

The boys were in the room with him, and it was evident that they realized what had happened. I could hear them clamoring.

"Is Mom OK?"

"Can the van make it home?"

And, finally, "If the van has had a wreck is it broken in? Will we be allowed to eat in it now?"

Yes, I suppose that it was truly broken in after my wreck. Now it was ready for French fries. What might have happened if the prayers hadn't made it to the Give Away box en route to our crash? Who knows? Prayer is a good thing to give away.

Asking for Prayer

We can ask other people to give away prayers for us. Long before I became a Christian, I believed in the power of prayer for the really big things. When I was in grade school, our kitchen caught on fire. I ran next door to Jane's house as her dad ran to ours to begin the fire-fighting process. I remember crying and telling Jane and her older sister to start praying so that our house didn't burn down.

It didn't and I probably failed to thank Him or to talk to Him again until the next consuming fire in my life.

Rhoda is a foster mother, one with a great big heart and lots of love. She's the kind of foster mom every kid in that position deserves. Through the years she and her husband have provided a home and love to many, many children. One special young lady moved in when she was just two days old; in fact, she has never lived anywhere else but in Rhoda's home.

After three and a half years as Rhoda's foster child, it seemed as if the girl was going to be adoptable, and Rhoda and her husband were definitely interested. They truly desired to make her a permanent, legal member of their family. The process was very long and very emotional. Sometimes weeks would pass without any positive change.

Our church prayed. Our women's Bible study prayed. Rhoda and her family prayed. We all prayed that her family would be able to adopt this little girl. One day, after a series of emotional ups and downs, Rhoda stopped me as I walked with a friend to my car after choir. She was almost at the end of her rope and she had a request to make of us.

"Do you remember in the Old Testament [Ex 17:8-16] when Moses held up his arms and the Lord's army prevailed? And then his arms became tired and he let them fall down and the Lord's army began to lose the battle? Do you know that passage?" she asked.

"Aaron and Hur came to Moses' aid. They came alongside of him and helped him hold up his arms to insure victory for the Israelites."

"Sure," we answered.

"I'm no Moses, but I don't think that I can hold up my arms one minute longer in this battle to adopt," she continued. "Would you two help me and hold up my arms?"

Of course the answer was yes and we pledged to pray daily for the Lord to work in the legal battle. In the family of God, we can ask for prayer. It was a privilege to pray each day for this little girl who would months later become the legal daughter of our dear friend.

Out of Order?

I know that prayer changes things because God's Word says so. I also know that I don't always pray in God's will. I occasionally take over and give God the directions.

Years ago I worked long and hard on a writing project and finally completed the task. When it was finished I mailed a portion of the manuscript to several publishers. Later that afternoon I drove to school to pick up Matthew, who was in junior high at the time.

"I completed my writing project and mailed the packages out today," I told him excitedly. "Now I want you to pray that God will bless it!"

"Let me get this straight," said the astute seventh grader. "You decided to write a book and now you want God to bless it."

He didn't have to go on. The little smartie was 100 percent right. I determined my direction and then I wanted God to bless it. I did not pray before starting the project to see if the endeavor was God's will. But after I was finished, I wanted God to touch it with His magic wand and give me my wishes.

God's Word says to delight in the Lord and He will give you

the desires of your heart (see Psalm 37:4-5). He gives us our desires because a committed life only desires what He wants to give. (By the way, do I need to tell you that my writing project was rejected?)

"Pretty! Shiny! Give me!" shrieks the toddler as he reaches for the carving knife on the counter. Do we give him what he wants? Of course not, because it is not the best for him. God, in His infinite knowledge, always knows what is best for us.

Ultimate Communication

Prayer is talking and listening. It is communication. Betty, Matthew's preschool Sunday school teacher, knelt at the altar to pray after taking communion.

"What's Betty doin'?" Matthew asked in a stage whisper even Betty could hear.

"She's talking to Jesus," was my reply and I put my finger to my lips as a signal to him. My nonverbal communication was not powerful enough and the inquisitive boy continued to probe.

"What's Jesus saying to her?" he asked in a voice even louder than before.

My answer came quickly as I attempted to silence him.

"I don't know," I replied. "She probably can't hear Jesus because of all the noise you are making."

He pondered that one long and hard and listened intently as others joined his Sunday school teacher at the altar to pray. Maybe he was trying to catch a little of their divine conversations.

In prayer we talk and we listen. That's how we fine-tune and refine our prayer. I am no expert on prayer, but I am a pray-er. Probably the most important thing I am beginning to understand about prayer is that I pray to *know* the mind of Christ not to *change* the mind of Christ. The more I understand what God desires for me and for those on my prayer list, the more effective my prayers will be.

Unselfish Prayers

Pam is a prayer warrior. What a great attribute for a friend to have! She is in the chapter "Choose to Pray" in my book *Empowered by Choice*. As I did research for that chapter, I asked her if she would share her prayer journal with me. What did I discover? As her daughter Emily faced surgery for an inoperable brain tumor, Pam's prayer list looked something like this:

Emily – healing from her tumor

Russ and Jeannette – marriage problems

Keith – knee surgery

Jill – needs a job after moving

I read entries like this day after day and I was amazed. I was also a little ashamed as I wondered if my prayer journal would be such a generous reflection of putting prayer in the Give Away box. It is possible that my journal would record that I was only focused on my own need, especially at such a perilous time.

Rita had a very difficult person in her life. She told me that for years and years she prayed for the person's salvation to no avail. Then one day she had a thought that was bigger than she could have thought all on her own.

"As I prayed that day for her salvation," Rita said, "God revealed to me that my motives were wrong. I wanted this woman to become a Christian to make my life easier. I didn't care about her eternal life at all. I only cared about the comfort of my temporal life."

What an insight. From that point on, Rita's heart was changed and so was her motivation. She discovered that, as she gave away unselfish prayers for this woman, she began to feel compassion and love where there had only been indifference. Prayer can change the pray-er.

Praying for someone can be general or specific. Sometimes I know the needs of an individual and sometimes I just know there is a need. For example, one particular week at college was no fun at all for Matthew. He called home on Thursday evening and outlined some of the things that had happened. When we hung up the phone I didn't know how to pray for him, so I generally lifted him and his concerns to God.

In the morning, I told John that I didn't know how to specifically pray for Matthew. John said he had been contemplating the exact same question and had decided to pray that Matthew would somehow be encouraged. That sounded good to me and I too began to pray that specific request. That evening I called Matthew, as we had agreed the night before, to make arrangements with him to come home for the remainder of the weekend. With a little hesitation, I asked him how his day had gone.

"It went pretty good," he said. "I was a little late for my

math class and when I came in some guys I knew hollered at me to come down front and sit with them. They really encouraged me."

When I heard the word *encouraged*, precisely what we had prayed for, I was so glad those prayers had filled the Give Away box. I didn't say anything to Matthew at the time, but my heart praised God. The person we are praying for doesn't necessarily have to know we are praying.

Are You Listening?

Once there was a young pastor who had a lot to learn, but he loved Jesus and had a teachable spirit. One day a little old lady from his congregation made an appointment to see him. As it turned out, her plan for the meeting was to straighten out the pastor.

After about thirty minutes of correction and criticism taken graciously by the pastor, he informed his visitor that he would need to close their meeting in order to make another appointment he had scheduled.

"Would you like me to pray before we leave?" asked the pastor.

"I think I'd rather do the praying," was the reply, "if that's all right with you."

"Certainly," he said. "That would be fine." And with that the parishioner wasted no time at all.

"Dear God," she began. "Help brother Tim to do a better job with visiting like I told him. And give him better sermon illustrations for his shorter sermons. And God, make him a little snappier dresser (and his wife too), and remind him to turn up the thermostat first thing on Sunday. Amen."

She unfolded her hands, raised her bowed head, and looked directly at her pastor. "Well, preacher," she said. "Did you hear what I just said?"

"Oh, I'm so sorry," he replied. "I wasn't listening. I thought you were talking to God."

I've often wondered if that permanently ended his counseling sessions with her.

Effectual and Fervent

God's Word tells us that the effectual, fervent prayer of a righteous person brings results (see James 5:16). On a few instances in my life I have been assured that people were giving away prayer for me. Occasionally the groups I speak to have an intercessor assigned to pray before, during, and after my presentation.

Once I flew to Florida to speak at a day-long teachers' institute. It was a wonderful experience. The teachers were such a good audience and so easy to speak to. One woman in particular was an encourager to me. At the break and at lunch she came up to visit with me and to share a story or two that supported the information I had given the group. A few weeks after the event I received a letter from her. Although the event was sponsored by a public school district, she had concluded that I was a Christian and hence her sister in Christ. (Thank goodness it showed.)

After a page and a half of encouragement and joy, Zona wrote, "I have added your name and ministry to our church prayer list. Also, a very special group of prayer warriors lift you before the Lord on Monday mornings." What a gift from this Christian friend!

My husband prays for me every day. This is a gift of love. Jesus also prays for me. "Therefore he [Jesus] is able to save completely those who come to God through him, because he always lives to intercede for them" (Heb 7:25). The Holy Spirit prays for me too.

In the same way, the Spirit helps us in our weakness. We do not know what we ought to pray, but the Spirit himself intercedes for us with groans that words cannot express. And he who searches our hearts knows the mind of the Spirit, because the Spirit intercedes for the saints in accordance with God's will.

ROMANS 8:26-27

Reflection

Do you give away prayer for your family? Write down one concern for each family member and pray for that concern each day for a week.

When did God answer a prayer you gave away for someone else?

Knowing that someone is praying for you is very exciting and comforting. Take time today to tell someone that you prayed for him or her.

There are many wonderful books on prayer including, of course, the Bible. Begin or continue your search for knowledge on prayer.

Chapter 12

The Give Away Rule

The Give Away box was getting very full. When this project began I never imagined I had so many things inside of me to give away. Is your Give Away box full too?

Treasures, Not Trash

Before we put this box aside, there is a rule you need to know. A little German lady, alias Mom, raised me, and she had a rule for almost everything. Mom always told me to make sure I only put things into the Give Away box that were useful to others. Don't give away junk; give away jewels. Don't give away garbage; give away good things. Don't give away trash; give away treasures.

How many of you have a closet filled to overflowing with once-upon-a-time treasures? Those polyester pantsuits used to be a fashion statement. But that was years and years ago. Fringed vests went out with the election of Jimmy Carter. And even though platform shoes are once again a hit, the new ones don't look like those old ones in your closet.

Do you really want to put that old toaster into the Give Away box? The repairman said it couldn't be fixed. And the avocado throw pillows with filling that has long since gone bad will probably do little to enhance someone else's home.

When I was dejunking my room as a young girl and I came to a giant 500-piece puzzle with several pieces missing, I would remember Mom's rule. Give away good things, not garbage. Her rule kept me from putting trash into the Give Away box. Instead it went into the Throw Away box.

"Why give away things someone else will just have to throw away?" she would ask. "Give away things people will appreciate, while they can be appreciated."

I remember when the time came to give away my sons' baby clothes. For me, this assignment was a difficult one. In fact, I was almost silly about it. We had three healthy boys and I was in my late thirties. The chances were slim that we would have another child.

"Why don't you get rid of the baby clothes?" John asked one day as he stared at the mountains of black garbage bags.

"I just hate to," I replied. "What if we have another baby?"

"If we have another baby," John said, confident that it was well beyond a long shot, "I'll buy him new clothes."

He was willing to take this very safe gamble in order to regain the use of several square feet of attic space. So I agreed.

Although I've been told that having a garage sale is fun, I've never been convinced of it. So rather than price the precious hand-me-downs, I sorted through the bags in order to retrieve special items for remembrances and to be sure no throw-away items were included. There was no reason to give away little shirts that were impossible to get clean or little trousers that were worn beyond repair.

As I sorted and sifted through the bags, I cried. The little socks and undershirts, pants, and one-piece outfits reminded me of an earlier time, a time that was gone and would never reappear. The things reminded me of change—something that is neither all bad nor all good. It is, however, inevitable. My boys were changing and growing almost daily and it was time to share these bags of clothes with someone else. It was time to put them into the Give Away box. In order to feel better as I worked on the task before me, I imagined what would transpire when the bags were opened and the treasures were removed from the Give Away box.

"Oh, look at this little shirt," the mother-to-be would exclaim. "It is so tiny!"

"And look at this beautiful blue suit," her mother would respond. "Your little guy will look so handsome in this!"

"And these blankets are so soft ... and just like new," the young woman would continue. "These things are exactly what I need."

Experience Needed

The same rule applies to the things that go from our hearts, minds, and memories into the Give Away box. When we spring clean our hearts, we must put the items into the correct box.

We have all had experiences that have no positive worth to another person. Perhaps every now and then we have the urge to share an experience for our own selfish gain. Maybe giving away that experience will illustrate how smart, talented, or extraordinary we are (or think we are). Maybe our desire in giving away the experience is to elevate ourselves.

I tend to be a person who gives away much more information than was actually requested. When I hear your answering machine ask for my name, number, and a brief message, I am able to ignore the word *brief*. After I left a message on someone's machine one day, my son confronted me and reminded me that it was not necessary to leave an "epic novel."

That epic novel might have contained information that was of no particular worth to the listener. I might have mentioned where I was going or where I had been or how my latest book was coming along. Usually I share those experiences because I am genuinely excited about them. Occasionally I include the information because I hope the listener will be excited too. The truth is that they probably don't care. In fact, by sharing these unsolicited experiences, I run the risk of puffing myself up in their eyes and giving them trash.

I am learning to control the giving away of experiences. If the experience is of no use to the listener, it is best to avoid putting it into the Give Away box. Remember to give away experience and wisdom as they are requested.

Sometimes the experience we give away puts us in a good light and someone else in a poor light. This is always destructive and definitely breaks the Give Away Rule. Do not give away experiences that could hurt another person.

Memory Lane

The memories we create also have the potential to be good things or garbage. Granted, we cannot always create a wonderful memory for our family or friends, but if a positive memory is our goal, at least we are aiming at the correct target.

My husband has been known to say, "Kendra never has a disaster, just another story to tell." That is pretty accurate, although one time I came very close to disaster and so did our boys. My memory of the event still causes me to shudder just a little.

In the summer of 1997 our family had the treat of an Alaskan vacation. As a part of that trip, we spent three days at Denali National Park. It was a spectacular location and we were enjoying everything about the trip. Early one morning we boarded a bus with several other park visitors and took an eight-hour trip back into the tundra wilderness to see the wildlife. As amazing as it might sound, all five of us were actually amused for the entire trip. We saw sheep, elk, and—the highlight—a great big grizzly bear. Our buses were stopped, and the tundra native simply ignored us as he lumbered down a creek bank, actually crossing the road between the two buses. We were very excited and snapped several photos of this massive bear. Our trip was now complete. We had seen a grizzly, up close and personal. Little did we realize that this session with a bear would soon pale in our memory.

After the bus tour ended, we drove to a large rock formation and did some climbing. Then we headed down the gradual slope to the riverbed. It was a braided river, which meant that rather than one stream there were multiple tributaries and tiny branches, which were braided together.

The boys began skipping rocks and walking upstream—the two older boys easily jumping over the narrow alleys of water as they went, and Jonathan jumping as far as he could and keeping as dry as he could. John and I climbed back up the slope and rested at a picnic table about three hundred yards from the river.

As we sat there visiting and enjoying the gorgeous scenery, a car drove up rather hurriedly. A man jumped from the car. "There are two grizzly bears running down the riverbed," he yelled.

His commentary on the wildlife did not register with either John or me.

"There are two male grizzlies in the riverbed, coming this way," he repeated, even more agitated.

When he did not get a satisfactory reply from us he continued with even more urgency, "Are those your kids down there? The bears are running right toward them!" Finally his message registered!

John left my side and raced toward the boys, yelling to get their attention. The wind was in his face and the boys were looking down at the river and could not hear him. He continued to run and yell, and now I could see the first bear coming.

Jonathan saw his dad first. He didn't know what John was saying, but he knew something was wrong and ran toward him. Aaron looked up as he saw Jonathan run by, and then he saw his dad and heard only one word, *BEAR*. That, combined with the panicked look on his dad's face, was enough of a clue for him. He took off like a gazelle toward safety.

Matthew, who was the farthest upstream, still had not responded to his father's cry. Oblivious to the fact that his brothers were running away from him and from imminent danger, he looked up in the direction of now two bears. One glance at the galloping grizzlies sent him in rapid pursuit of safety. Within seconds he caught up to Aaron. As he ran beside him, he actually pointed out that all the books recommended you stand completely still if a bear approaches.

"Fine," Aaron replied, panting. "Then he'll eat you first!"

By this time the first bear was about fifty feet from the boys and suddenly veered to the left and took off up the mountainside. The second bear followed, as his mission was to chase bear number one from his territory.

Only seconds later the boys and their dad reached my side. Do I need to tell you that I was extremely emotional by that time? We stood together and watched the two huge grizzly bears as they continued the chase up the slope and finally moved out of sight. As I was praising God for the protection and trying to regain my composure, the boys became a little emotional too. Their emotion, however, was not fear or relief, but sheer exhilaration.

"Wow, that was great," said Aaron.

"Did you see how close that first bear got?" asked Matthew.

"And I didn't have any trouble jumping those streams," added Jonathan.

They had survived the near-attack and they were loving it. A disaster? Absolutely not! That five minutes was one of the highlights of the trip. A memory was created that none of us will ever forget. (Our only risk with the bear memory is that each son will distort it to magnify his own heroic efforts.) It became a great memory almost instantaneously for the boys, and little by little I am enjoying the remembrance.

When a positive memory is your goal, you are aiming at the right target. With a sense of adventure and a sense of humor, many memories can become good ones to give away.

Jewels or Junk?

Encouragement is hardly ever misconstrued as junk. It is almost always a jewel. Perhaps the only time it might warrant a trip to the Throw Away box instead of the Give Away box is when it is insincere.

If you assure me that my red hair is truly lovely and I have brown hair, your encouraging words will definitely be suspect. Encouragement must be genuine and have no ulterior motives to belong in the Give Away box.

Recently I was reminded, in a backdoor sort of way, of the importance of giving away genuine, honest encouragement. I was speaking to about 120 women at a luncheon for women in management. My message had been well received and the noon-hour meeting had been by many standards a success. I was gathering my props and the leftover handouts when the president of the group came over to converse with me.

Her kind words were very positive and encouraging and she closed her comments with an interesting thought.

"I want you to know that even though I am in public relations, you can trust my words," she said. "I am concerned people will think that I'm always putting a spin on the situation."

Her encouragement came with an interesting disclaimer: In spite of how I have been trained, these words are true. If encouragement is given away for the sole purpose of advancing a cause, the encouragement will not be sincere or effective.

Faith in Jesus Christ and prayer are good things to give away when the emphasis is on Jesus. If *my* faith, *my* belief, *my* power in prayer are the emphases, then even giving away our faith can be destructive.

To some who were confident of their own righteousness and looked down on everybody else, Jesus told this parable: "Two men went up to the temple to pray, one a Pharisee and the other a tax collector. The Pharisee stood up and prayed about himself: 'God, I thank you that I am not like other men—robbers, evildoers, adulterers—or even like this tax collector. I fast twice a week and give a tenth of all I get.'

"But the tax collector stood at a distance. He would not even look up to heaven, but beat his breast and said, 'God, have mercy on me, a sinner.'

"I tell you that this man, rather than the other, went home justified before God. For everyone who exalts himself will be humbled, and he who humbles himself will be exalted."

LUKE 18:9-14

When my desire is to elevate me or to illustrate my superior spiritual nature, even faith and prayer turn from jewels to junk, from good things to garbage, from treasures to trash.

In my travels I have experienced many different forms of worship. Typically I am able to feel comfortable in any type of service as long as the emphasis is on Jesus. On one particular evening, however, I attended a "religious" meeting that left me feeling far from "religious."

I arrived a little early for the service and was encouraged to explore the facility. As I wandered behind the stage area, I came upon one of the leaders for the evening speaking very unkindly to another person. In fact, she was giving him a real tongue-lashing. Not intending to eavesdrop on this rude reprimand, I immediately turned around to go into the sanctuary.

The words that I had inadvertently overheard were very disconcerting, and my shock and disgust grew as this same woman came to the podium to begin the service.

"Good evening, brothers and sisters," she began. "I am here to lead you in praise and worship to our Lord."

I couldn't imagine how that same mouth that had just torn apart one of her contemporaries was now going to lead me in worship. The letter of James talks about this very problem: "With the tongue we praise our Lord and Father, and with it we curse men, who have been made in God's likeness. Out of the same mouth come praise and cursing. My brothers, this should not be" (3:9-10).

So I have to pay attention as I sort the clutter in my heart. I want the Give Away box to be as full as I can get it, but I don't want throw-away items to sneak into it. As you spring clean your heart, remember the rule for the Give Away box.

Reflection

When you give away your experiences, can you see how God could use them for good? Have you ever used the giving away of your experiences to manipulate someone else? (Don't slide over that hard question.) If you can think of a time when that happened, admit it and ask God for forgiveness. And remember to give away treasures in the future.

It is important to give away jewels, not junk. Otherwise we are merely contributing to the negative clutter in someone else's heart. Has anyone ever given you something that should have been put into the Throw Away box instead? How long did you trip over it before you realized it was only garbage? Let this experience serve as a reminder to you to give away good things.

Chapter 13

Let's Keep These Things

My Keep box was the smallest of the three boxes. Amazingly, I had found several things for the Give Away box. I had filled the Throw Away box to overflowing, and now it was time to determine what I should keep. As I sorted the remaining items, I realized that there was a very important thing I had inside of me that I wanted to keep.

I wanted to keep God's Word. This certainly did not cause clutter in my heart, mind, and memory. In fact, in many ways, it helped to eliminate clutter and could actually keep my heart free of junk.

Hide It in Your Heart

Let me give you an example. In Psalm 119:11 we are told that hiding God's Word in our hearts (putting it into the Keep box) will help keep us from sin. Sin is a definite cause of clutter. Putting God's Word in the Keep box can help prevent that sinful clutter.

The young woman knew that she was making a poor choice. She was so sure that her actions were wrong, in fact, that she made a conscious decision to avoid thinking about her choices or evaluating their appropriateness. What was she doing? She was flirting with a young man at work. Actually, she was flirting with adultery, for she was a married woman.

"I'm not doing anything wrong," she would argue with herself when her conscience was pricked by her behavior. "He's just a friend, that's all. There's nothing wrong with having a friend."

And so the "friendship" grew. They would take time to visit each day at their 10:00 coffee break, and eventually they started eating lunch together. Occasionally the woman would have pangs of guilt and doubt that what she was doing was wise. Usually she was able to stifle those doubts and convince herself that the meetings she was having with the "other man" were innocent.

Then one day she was feeling particularly bad about the relationship that was growing. She sought counsel in order to help her sort through her feelings. Unfortunately she did not listen to Psalm 1, guidance for anyone seeking counsel.

> Blessed is the man
> who does not walk in the counsel of the wicked
> or stand in the way of sinners
> or sit in the seat of mockers.
> But his delight is in the law of the Lord,
> and on his law he meditates day and night.
>
> PSALM 1:1-2

This woman sought the counsel of another woman whose behavior did not reflect the wisdom of Scripture. Instead of delighting in the law of the Lord, the flirting woman found a counselor whose lifestyle mimicked the poor decisions she wanted to continue. She got the advice she wanted and it ultimately ended her career with that corporation and almost ended her marriage.

Hiding God's Word in your heart can help to keep you from sin. "Direct my footsteps according to your word; let no sin rule over me" (Ps 119:133).

Your Weapon of Choice

The Word of God is described as a sword. "Take the helmet of salvation and the sword of the Spirit, which is the word of God" (Eph 6:17). God's Word is our offensive weapon in the battle with the enemy. Jesus Himself used the Word to battle Satan.

Then Jesus was led by the Spirit into the desert to be tempted by the devil. After fasting forty days and forty nights, he was hungry. The tempter came to him and said, "If you are the Son of God, tell these stones to become bread."

Jesus answered, "It is written: 'Man does not live on bread alone, but on every word that comes from the mouth of God.'"

MATTHEW 4:1-4

Jesus knew the Word of God and pulled His sword to quote from Deuteronomy 8:3. The devil decided that two could use the power of the Word, but in his arrogance he tried to battle with the One who was the Word (see John 1:1).

> Then the devil took him to the holy city and had him stand
> on the highest point of the temple. "If you are the Son of
> God," he said, "throw yourself down. For it is written: 'He
> will command his angels concerning you, and they will lift
> you up in their hands, so that you will not strike your foot
> against a stone.'"
>
> Jesus answered him, "It is also written: 'Do not put the
> Lord your God to the test.'"
>
> MATTHEW 4:5-7

Jesus had gone to the Word of God to fight Satan with the
message of Deuteronomy 6:16. Then we read:

> Again, the devil took him to a very high mountain and
> showed him all the kingdoms of the world and their splen-
> dor. "All this I will give you," he said, "if you will bow down
> and worship me."
>
> Jesus said to him, "Away from me, Satan! For it is written:
> 'Worship the Lord your God, and serve him only.'"
>
> MATTHEW 4:8-10

Jesus had answered with 1 Chronicles 21:1, and the Word of
God, which is the Sword of the Spirit, won the battle. "Then
the devil left him, and angels came and attended him" (Mt
4:11).

Unfortunately I have witnessed times when the Word was
used as a lethal weapon directed toward others rather than

toward evil. I have seen Scripture quoted not to remind the speaker or the listener of the truth but to impress, depress, or repress the listener. That is not the weapon that God intended His Word to be.

Encouragement Extraordinaire

I want to keep the Word in my heart in order to keep me from sin and to equip me for battle. Additionally, God's Word can go into the Keep box to encourage us.

My husband and I teach an adult Sunday school class. He is the primary instructor and it is my job to supply an occasional appropriate anecdote and make sure everyone feels loved. (I have the easy job.) One Sunday he announced to our class of about twelve people that not only were we going to study encouragement this quarter, but each one of us was also going to memorize Psalm 139. The looks on everyone's faces said it all.

"Memorize?"

"You're kidding!"

"I can't."

"You're kidding!!"

"I won't."

"You're kidding!!!"

"I'm too old."

"Tell me you're kidding."

"We're not going to have a quiz on this, are we?"

John assured the class that there would be no quiz and no class presentation during the worship service. He let us know that we were going to commit this chapter of the Old Testament to memory (hide it in our hearts) because it was so encouraging. He then proceeded to draw a verbal picture for us of the first two verses. His picture made memorizing the verses very easy. I will be keeping this psalm in my heart, mind, and memory.

The Perfect Instructor

The Word of God is a "lamp to my feet and a light for my path" (Ps 119:105). It illuminates my path, keeping me from sin, equipping me for spiritual battle, encouraging me, and it also gives me instruction.

Paul wrote, "Whatever is true, whatever is noble, whatever is right, whatever is pure, whatever is lovely, whatever is admirable—if anything is excellent or praiseworthy—think about such things" (Phil 4:8). Christ is all those things. When we attended our Lamaze classes before the birth of our first child, we were told, among other things, to decide on something specific to focus on during labor. I chose to picture the face of Jesus as I had seen it depicted in paintings ("think about such things").

Conversely, whatever is untrue, whatever is dishonorable, whatever is inappropriate, whatever is impure, whatever is hideous, whatever is contemptible—if anything is inferior or disreputable—do *not* think about such things. I think Zig Ziglar would call that last list "stinkin' thinkin'." And that is to be avoided. God's Word tells us that as a man "thinks in his heart, so he is" (Prv 23:7a, NKJV). Our thoughts are very important. The items we keep and dwell upon have great influence over us.

Picture This

Putting God's Word into the Keep box also ensures that I will have an accurate picture of God. We have all heard stories of how little children describe God. Some of their descriptions are humorous. Some are farfetched and some are remarkably accurate.

"I don't know too much about God," the preschooler replied in answer to the request that she describe God. "All I know for sure is that His name is Howard. You know, 'Our Father who art in Heaven, Howard be Thy name.'"

Several years ago there was a popular cartoon called "Dear God" based on supposed letters from kids to God. The ideas were cute and reminded us of the fresh, uncultured way kids address the Lord, but they did not necessarily give an accurate picture of God. In order to get a factual picture of God it is important to determine who He is based on His Word.

God is the creator (see Genesis 1:1). He created all things (see Colossians 1:16), including us in His image (see Genesis 1:27). He can create love where there is no love and restore a marriage which seems destined for demise. He can create life and bless a husband and wife with a child.

I was in the grocery store and a woman came charging out of the produce section to show me a photo. It was a picture of the woman herself and a beautiful little baby girl. The baby, she explained, was going to be their daughter by the end of the month. She and her husband were adopting the little girl. God created life, and the little life in the picture would soon be in the arms of her mommy and daddy.

God is a jealous God (see Exodus 34:14). I want to be sure to give Him His place in my life. There are to be no other gods before Him (see Exodus 20:3). That includes my husband, our kids, my speaking and writing, money, or things. All of those can become gods. They can rise up the list of priorities until they are in the number one spot. That's not a good idea. We can't serve two masters.

God is merciful (see Deuteronomy 4:31). He is gracious and compassionate (see 2 Chronicles 30:9). He is forgiving (see Nehemiah 9:17). He is righteous (see Romans 1:17). He is faithful (see 1 Corinthians 10:13). He is spirit (see John 4:24), light (see 1 John 1:5), and love (see 1 John 4:16). What a wonderful picture! God is all those things and more. He blesses us, disciplines us, and is our refuge (see Deuteronomy 15:6; 8:5; 33:27).

I remember when a young man in our youth group got a better picture of the true nature of God. We had taken twenty teenagers to a conference at a big city about two hours from home. The two-day event was a great way to achieve both spiritual growth for the young people of our church and sleep deprivation for young and old. (I was in the latter category.)

As the kids piled into my van for the trip home, they were welcomed on board with a very typical greeting.

"Now," I began, "everyone think of one thing that you learned over the last two days. I want you to share at least one thing that really affected you."

My youth group kids are used to these "reflective sessions" and they are also used to humoring me by participating. So each teenager thought about my challenge and prepared to give me an insight they had received during the conference.

One girl told me about the main points from a purity workshop she had attended. One of my riders talked about the worship and the teen-friendly songs that were sung. And finally John, one of our youth group officers, spoke up.

"You know what hit me?" John asked. "It was something the main speaker said about a passage in Psalms. Wait, I wrote down the verses. Let me look it up. 'How precious to [or concerning] me are your thoughts, O God! How vast is the sum of them! Were I to count them, they would outnumber the grains of sand. When I awake, I am still with you.' What an awesome thing! God's thoughts concerning me are so numerous that they outnumber the grains of sand! That's a lot of thoughts. He cares for me *that* much."

From Psalm 139:17-18 John had a glimpse of the accurate picture of God and His love for each one of us. He realized that God was so filled with love and concern for him that He thought of him countless times. That is an awesome and accurate picture of God. The picture came from the Word of God.

Too many times our picture of our heavenly Father is influenced by our picture of our earthly father and is not necessarily accurate. No earthly father can adequately portray our perfect heavenly Father. Some earthly fathers have no attributes which even resemble God. To be accurate, our picture must be based on the Bible.

"Comfort Ye My People"

Comfort also comes from having God's Word in the Keep box.

We visited Pat in the hospital. She was very ill—too ill, in fact, to even realize that we were there. But her folks appreciated the company and the break from their bedside vigil. Pat's body was filled with tumors. She had lost a considerable amount of weight and the cancerous lumps were visible all over her body.

Her thin hospital gown was uncomfortable for her as it lay on the tumors on her thighs and torso. With her hands at her side, she slowly and deliberately gathered up her gown to relieve the pressure it presented. Underneath the gown she was naked and, as the gown inched up to her midsection, her mom gently pulled it down to give Pat some modesty.

In her pain, modesty did not matter. As soon as her gown was pulled down and smoothed over her body, she began again to hike it up.

"It's OK," I told her mother. "Just so Pat is as comfortable as she can be."

Evidently that was the assurance her mother needed and she left the gown gathered around Pat's midsection. As we left, seeing her alive for the last time, God's Word blared in my ear.

Who shall separate us from the love of Christ? Shall trouble or hardship or persecution or famine or nakedness or danger or sword? As it is written: "For your sake we face death all day long; we are considered as sheep to be slaughtered." No, in all these things we are more than conquerors through him who loved us. For I am convinced that neither death nor life, neither angels nor demons, neither the present nor the future, nor any powers, neither height nor depth, nor anything else in all creation, will be able to separate us from the love of God that is in Christ Jesus our Lord.

ROMANS 8:35-39

Pat, a young woman who loved Jesus, would never be separated from Him. God's Word comforted me that day. It will comfort us as we keep it in our hearts, minds, and memories.

Promises, Promises

The verses that comforted me that day also gave me a promise, one that will never disappoint. By putting God's Word into the Keep box, I am able to keep the promises of God in my heart. They are all enumerated in the Scriptures.

God's promises are different from the promises I make. Although I may try my best to always keep my word, chances are that I will sometimes fail. I may not remember a promise or I may be unable to honor a promise because of circumstances I had not anticipated or that were beyond my control.

God always keeps His Word. It is flawless (see Proverbs 30:5) and it will stand forever (see Isaiah 40:8). God's promises are guaranteed:

"For God so loved the world that he gave his one and only Son, that whoever believes in him shall not perish but have eternal life" (Jn 3:16). What a wonderful promise of God! If I believe in God's one and only Son, Jesus, then I will have eternal life.

"Do not be anxious about anything, but in everything, by prayer and petition, with thanksgiving, present your requests to God. And the peace of God, which transcends all understanding, will guard your hearts and your minds in Christ Jesus" (Phil

4:6-7). All I have to do is to exchange anxiety for thankful prayer.

God's promises never change because He never changes. "Jesus Christ is the same yesterday and today and forever" (Heb 13:8). And He keeps His promises. Putting God's Word into the Keep box means that I have the means to stay away from sin, the weapon to fight in spiritual battles, a source of encouragement and instruction, an accurate picture of God Himself, comfort, and the knowledge of His promises. These are good things to keep! Ponder the following passages:

"Praise the Lord. Blessed is the man who fears the Lord, who finds great delight in his commands" (Ps 112:1).

"I will never forget your precepts, for by them you have renewed my life" (Ps 119:93).

"The grass withers and the flowers fall, but the word of our God stands forever" (Is 40:8).

Reflection

Do you have parts of God's Word hidden in your heart? See if you can recite some of the Bible. Now commit to memorizing more. Maybe you'd like to join our Sunday school class on Psalm 139.

Are you guilty of "stinkin' thinkin'"? Check out Philippians 4:8 and think on those things.

What picture do you have of God? In twenty-five words or less describe God.

How did you do? Did your description match up with the Word of God?

Chapter 14

The Keep Paradox

I realized as I gently put God's Word into the Keep box that many of the things I had put into the Give Away box I could actually keep too. It was a paradox.

Response or Reaction?

I have learned from experience that it is wiser to respond than to react in a situation. By my definition, a response is a thinking reply and a reaction is similar to a knee jerk (no thinking there).

I have obtained this wisdom from both positive and negative experiences. In one particular incident, I was reminded of the wisdom of responding by failing to do it.

Our family took a vacation one summer to New York City. Because we live on a farm in central Illinois, this adventure was very different from our daily lives.

On the few days we spent in the city, we did all the typical tourist things including a trip to the Empire State Building. After that particular excursion, we walked across the street to dine at ... McDonald's! I've heard that there are some unforgettable spots for dining in the Big Apple, but on that special night our choice was to eat in a setting reminding us of home.

We stood in line behind a group of young Italians who apparently spoke no English. It was fascinating to watch them pantomime "Big Mac" and "French fry."

After our overseas visitors obtained their order, the woman behind the counter looked at me, as the mother of the group, and gave me the traditional McDonald's head nod. It means "Go ahead. You are next. I'm ready for your order."

As I opened my mouth to say, "Number two, please (with an orange drink)," a man who had merged into our line spoke up. We recognized him immediately as a security guard at the Empire State Building. This uniformed and armed diner interrupted me in mid-sentence.

"I'm next," he said gruffly and to no one in particular.

His interruption startled me and I instantly stopped repeating our order. The woman behind the counter didn't seem to be startled or even very surprised. "No, you're not," she said calmly to the rude man. "This lady is next. Go ahead, Lady." And simultaneous to her statement she once again gave me "the nod."

I started again, a little more tentatively this time.

"I'd like a number two..."

That was as far as I got before the security guard interrupted again. "Hey," he shouted menacingly, "I said I was next!"

Still unruffled, the McDonald's employee shook her head in disagreement and turned back to me. This was all it took to send the highly impatient security guard into a shouting fit. He yelled obscenities that I had never even imagined before, much less heard. He called the woman behind the counter ugly, disrespectful names and shouted these crude things with increasing volume.

I was shocked. My reactions took over. With no thinking whatsoever I quickly leaned forward across the McDonald's counter. I reached my hand to pat the arm of our order taker and very loudly told her that *"no one* deserves to be talked to in that manner." I wanted to be sure that the guard knew I disapproved of his colorful vocabulary.

What I had forgotten was that (1) this was New York City (not East Lynn, Illinois) and (2) this man I was trying to correct was armed with a gun.

As I was leaning and patting and chastising the ill-mannered security guard, my kids were tugging at me and trying to get me to stop. Can you see the potential headline? "Midwestern Woman Gunned Down by Security Guard in Downtown McDonald's!" I'm sure it would have been assumed that he felt I was a threat to security. In actuality, I was merely reacting to his bad behavior and foul mouth.

Thank goodness that headline never made the paper. Instead he turned around and left. I was safe in spite of my actions. As I reflected on the incident, I realized how foolish I had been. It reinforced my commitment to respond in a situation rather than react. I had learned from experience. I could put this experience into the Give Away box and I could keep it too.

Recycled Memories

Memories fit the paradox too. They can be put into the Give Away box and also remain in the Keep box. In chapter 8 I described how the Fat Fairy performed many acts of kindness in our home. I also let you in on the "secret" that I am actually the official Fat Fairy. I am the official one, but I am not the first one.

I grew up in a home that was frequented by the Fat Fairy. She left money for teeth that I had lost, she hid the Easter eggs, and she presented our family with one or two gifts under the Christmas tree each year. Come to think about it, the Fat Fairy almost always left a gift for my mom. She is a wonderful memory that I have from my childhood. So I put it into the Give Away box for my boys to enjoy. I also got to keep it for myself.

Encouragement to Give Away and Keep

As I headed north and west on the Tri-State toll road around Chicago, the traffic was bumper to bumper. We never have those kinds of traffic problems where I live except maybe for a few minutes after the Sweet Corn Festival parade. People around big cities are used to the congestion and the ritual of stop-and-go driving as each driver pays the toll and travels down the road.

I didn't have exact change so I edged my way over to a manual lane. As I slowly approached the toll booth, I could see the woman who would take my dollar and give me change. Then it was my turn. I handed the woman a dollar bill and the most amazing thing happened. The toll booth lady spoke. This was highly unusual. Typically there was no conversation as the exchange of money was made, except for an occasional grunt in reply to my thank-you.

"Did you see that car in front of you?" she asked in a very disgruntled manner.

I knew immediately that this had to be a rhetorical question because his bumper had been inches from mine for at least a mile and a half. Before I could answer, she went on.

"Well," she continued, "he was talking on his cellular phone and he wanted a receipt. He did not even have the garaciousness to ask for one. He just continued his conversation and snapped his fingers at me."

At this point, I was awestruck. I was actually having a conversation with a toll booth lady. I knew this was history in the making and an event which would probably never be repeated. Simultaneous with this thought was the realization that I had merely a brief moment in which to reply. I had only seconds to encourage this woman who had been discouraged by the previous driver.

My mind raced and then it came to me. I looked up at her, extended my hand to receive my change, shook my head, and said, "My, my! What would his mama say?"

She thought for just an instant, then smiled and laughed at the thought of the rude driver's mother scolding him for his behavior.

It worked! She was encouraged. I put encouragement into the Give Away box and she took it out. Actually, we were both encouraged. She was encouraged to note that not all of mankind (or womankind) was rude and self-serving, and I was encouraged to note that I had encouraged her.

Keep the Faith (and Give It Away)

My brother-in-law lay in a hospital bed, dying from a cancerous brain tumor. Every other day I visited him and read to him. I filled his hospital room with Scripture verses and on every visit I prayed for him and with him.

One day, the chief oncology nurse asked to see me in an adjacent room. Her countenance let me know before a word was spoken that she had some serious business to discuss.

"You must stop praying for your brother-in-law to be healed," she began in a very dictatorial tone. "He is extremely ill and it is time that you faced reality."

I was momentarily shocked by this lecture. But rapidly I came to my senses.

"Do you know who Shadrach, Meshach, and Abednego are?" I asked in response.

Disgustedly she shook her head "no."

"Well," I continued, undaunted, "they were three men who lived in Old Testament times. These three men made the very unpopular decision not to bow down to an idol made by Nebuchadnezzar, the king of Babylon and ruler of the nation. This choice made Nebuchadnezzar unhappy (gross understatement) and he ordered the men to be thrown into a furnace if they would not cooperate and worship him.

"The three men were not interested in Nebuchadnezzar's

threats," I went on, "and told him so. They were thrown into the furnace because they continued to worship God. But that same God protected them and they came out of the fiery furnace unharmed."

After I finished my Bible lesson I tried to help this nurse see the analogy and my point. "The God I know and worship is very capable of healing my brother-in-law," I said, "because He can do anything He chooses to do. So I am asking Him to do that miracle. And even if He doesn't, I will not stop loving and serving Him. He is reality."

She sat across from me and stared in disbelief. The reality in my life and in my brother-in-law's life was the reality of Jesus Christ. I was choosing to celebrate life until there was no more earthly life. Then there would be plenty of time to grieve. "But even if he does not, we want you to know, O king, that we will not serve your gods or worship the image of gold you have set up" (Dan 3:18).

Only days before, I had shared my faith with my brother-in-law. I had put my faith into the Give Away box and he had snatched it out. The paradox was that I gave it away and I kept it too. I still had my faith to share with the nurse.

Unceasing Prayer

When we put prayer into the Give Away box, we typically speak to God on behalf of someone else. We give away intercessory prayer. We keep the knowledge of the power of prayer and the ability to speak with God over and over again—in intercessory prayer, in praise and adoration, in confession, in thanksgiving. Prayer is never "used up." There is no finite number of words or visits with God that we are allowed.

A college student volunteered to help a friend one day. This friend needed someone to baby-sit her seven-year-old daughter for several hours on Saturday afternoon. After two hours of serving as the resident adult, this college student was very exhausted. It seemed that the child in her charge was constantly talking. The incessant conversation was causing the sitter to grow increasingly weary.

Finally, after three hours of continual conversation, the desperate baby sitter got to the end of her rope. "Christina," she said, addressing the little girl, "did you know that you only get a limited number of words that you can use each day? I thought you might like to know that because you are using your words up really fast!"

The girl thought about this unusual (and deceptive) revelation and decided she had better be quiet awhile and save some words for later that afternoon when her mom got home. Needless to say, when Mom did arrive and learned about her daughter's newfound (and incorrect) information, she was not too happy.

The baby sitter was not telling her young ward the truth. There was no limit to the number of words the little girl could use that day or any other day (although there might have been a limit to the number of words the baby sitter could tolerate).

Likewise, there is no limit to the frequency with which we pray or the number of words we use to talk to God. We can put prayer into the Give Away box and still have plenty for the Keep box. I once heard a gentleman say, "When I get to heaven and find out just how much my effectual, fervent prayers *did* avail, I will wish I had prayed more."

Reflection

Have you learned something from your experiences that you can give away and keep? Perhaps you have had a similar experience with the choices of reacting or responding. Did you have a good experience or a bad experience that provided you with wisdom? You can put it into the Give Away box and into the Keep box too.

Name a memory you have that you want to give away to your children. The good news is that you can keep it too.

Think of a time when encouraging someone encouraged you. Jot it down.

Has your faith been bolstered as you gave it away to another who gladly embraced it? We can give away our faith and keep it.

Chapter 15

One More Rule

The task of dejunking my heart, mind, and memory was almost complete. The spring cleaning was going well and things were looking pretty clean inside of me. Boy, that was a step in the right direction.

Just as I was about to declare the task of cleaning up the clutter of my heart finished, I remembered one more rule that Mom had taught me. This rule was not unique. In fact, the chances are great that just as my mom taught this rule to me, your mom taught it to you, and you and I have taught or will teach it to our children.

Keep It Clean

What is the rule? When you get it clean, keep it clean. The logic is so obvious, yet the task itself is quite challenging. This was a great idea, but I found it very difficult.

Have any of you ever sorted through the clutter in the drawer by your refrigerator only to find that in six months or even in six weeks the drawer was a wreck again? How in the world are we supposed to keep it clean? One Sunday I received a real insight into the answer to that question: We can keep it clean by evaluating the clutter before we ever take it into our lives.

I was sitting in Sunday school and our teacher had just told us to open our Bibles to the passage for the morning lesson. I began to read and almost immediately I saw a parallel between it and my mom's rule.

Jesus entered Jericho and was passing through. A man was there by the name of Zacchaeus; he was a chief tax collector and was wealthy. He wanted to see who Jesus was, but being a short man he could not, because of the crowd. So he ran ahead and climbed a sycamore-fig tree to see him, since Jesus was coming that way.

When Jesus reached the spot, he looked up and said to him, "Zacchaeus, come down immediately. I must stay at your house today." So he came down at once and welcomed him gladly.

All the people saw this and began to mutter, "He has gone to be the guest of a 'sinner.'"

But Zacchaeus stood up and said to the Lord, "Look, Lord! Here and now I give half of my possessions to the poor, and if I have cheated anybody out of anything, I will pay back four times the amount."

LUKE 19:1-8

What did Zacchaeus' lunchtime meeting with Jesus have to do with the old adage "When you get it clean, keep it clean"?

Let's take a closer look at the Scripture. Zacchaeus heard that

Jesus was coming to town, but being "vertically challenged," he knew that he had to find a good spot if he hoped to see Jesus. He climbed up in a tree and not only did he see Jesus, but Jesus saw him. Was everyone pleased that Jesus had noticed and spoken to Zacchaeus? No way! The onlookers were hostile and called him a sinner. I guess they didn't realize that they were sinners too (see Romans 3:23).

"I have a roast in the oven, Jesus. Wouldn't you like to come over to my house for dinner?"

"I'm a good cook, Jesus. When we have potluck at church I never bring home any leftovers."

But Jesus chose to eat with Zacchaeus.

"I can't believe that Jesus would want to eat with Zacchaeus. He's a no-good, dirty tax collector."

"And I got new carpeting just this weekend. I had to pay a premium to get it installed in time. Now Jesus isn't even coming over. He's going to be the guest of that awful man."

What did Zacchaeus do in the midst of this muttering? He set a wonderful example for each one of us, an example of how to keep it clean. The possibility existed that the things the townspeople were muttering about were absolutely true. If their criticisms were accurate, Zacchaeus needed to examine his life and make some changes. These grumblers might have been putting helpful things into the Give Away box.

By the same token, it might have all been junk. They might have been giving him trash instead of treasures. The muttering might have belonged in the Throw Away box. Have you ever been criticized? If you haven't, I am assuming you are dead. (Which, by the way, does not necessarily exempt you from criticism.) Everyone has been criticized and sometimes it is something we need to pay attention to. It may be something we need to change in our lives. Other times, the criticism was merely someone else's stinking trash that they were putting into our lives.

We are back to the two very serious and difficult questions that hover over the dejunking and cast their dark shadows on the process.

Difficult question number one: What if I throw this item away and then discover that I need it? In the case of Zacchaeus, what if this criticism and muttering is valid and he chooses to ignore it?

Equally difficult question number two: What if I keep this item and it is only junk? What if Zacchaeus accepts all this muttering as true and takes it into his heart to add to the clutter?

What did the tax collector do? He had those two important questions to answer and he chose not to address the people who were muttering. Instead he took it straight to the top: "Look, Lord! Here and now I give half of my possessions to the poor, and if I have cheated anybody out of anything, I will pay back four times the amount."

Zacchaeus must have known that in order to keep it clean, he would need to ask the Lord about the truth. God knows if the muttering and criticism from others belongs in the Give Away box or in the Throw Away box. There is no need to address those who are muttering. We keep it clean by identifying the truth before we let the clutter into our hearts, minds, and memories.

Clutter Control

When I clear off my desk each day, I have the option of opening the top drawer and sliding all the clutter from my desktop directly into the drawer. If I shut it rapidly (providing that shutting it is even a possibility), I can convince myself that I have handled the junk. In reality, if I take the time to determine the appropriate spot for each item on my desktop and then put things where they belong, I am more likely to keep it clean.

Zacchaeus asked God to help him know where the clutter belonged. He wanted to put things where they should be. He wanted to get it clean and keep it clean. I don't always do what Zacchaeus did. Many times I try to reason with those who are muttering. I try to convince them of my innocence in the matter or to persuade them that their criticism is misdirected. This typically gets me nowhere.

It is far better to take it straight to the top. The Lord knows what we need to take into our hearts. He knows what changes we need to make. By the same token, He will protect us from things meriting the Throw Away box. Tell Him, "Look, Lord, if I have done this thing, if I have acted selfishly, if I have been arrogant and self-centered, if I have done anything from vain ambition or selfish conceit, then please tell me. Because I want to be a woman of God. I want to be more like you."

God loves you. In fact, He is crazy about you and He only wants the best for you. We know that, for we have put God's Word in the Keep box so we know His true nature. When He prunes and nudges us, it is done lovingly and gently and it is for our good. God loves you and wants you to succeed.

By the same token, if He lets you know that some or all of the muttering is not relevant or applicable, you know you don't have to let the clutter into your life. Instead, it belongs in the Throw Away box. If you bring it into your heart and it is only trash, you will just have to sort through it later and throw it out.

Take it straight to the top and let the Lord guide you. Zacchaeus has given us a great example of this. God will help you get it clean and keep it clean.

Reflection

Recall a time when you were the subject of muttering (sometimes in the guise of "constructive criticism"). Did you take all of it in? Did you reject it all? Sort through the muttering by taking your concern straight to the top. Seek the mind of Christ on the issue.

Conclusion

The job is complete ... at least for now. Perhaps with concerted effort and an eye to Zacchaeus' example, I will be able to keep it clean. At least I will be able to sort a portion of the clutter before I allow it into my heart.

In the future I will be accumulating more and more treasures that I can give away. My experiences increase with each passing day, as does wisdom (gained from good and poor responses to those experiences).

Each day allows me the opportunity to create a new memory. My aging mother grieves her occasional loss of short-term memory ("I wrote things on a list and now I can't find the list"), yet her long-term memory is sterling and many times comforts and amuses her. Memories are good things to give away.

So is encouragement. I am convinced that encouragement is available in a never-ending supply. We do not need to ration it in fear that we only have a limited quantity. The more encouragement we give away, the more we seem to have to give away.

Faith and our faith experiences increase also. That means

more to give away and more to keep. Betty, a missionary whom my husband's family has known for years, is typically greeted by John asking, "What has Jesus been doing in your life lately?" And she returns the question.

Our faith is not static, it is active. In the words of the song, "We serve a risen Savior. He's in the world today." In one week I will have new accounts of God at work in my life and in the lives of those around me. There is always something current about our faith we can give away.

The prayers we give away will never be depleted. The Bible tells us to pray without ceasing, so it is obvious that the reservoir is deep. We are to pray at all times. This doesn't mean we must fold our hands and bow our head twenty-four hours a day. It means we are to have a God-consciousness twenty-four hours a day. We are to be conscious of God in every aspect of our lives. He is not to be compartmentalized for notice on Sunday only. Praying without ceasing—having a God-consciousness—means that decisions, conversations, and actions will all be done knowing God is present.

So many things can be given away and so many can be kept at the same time. And always remember to give away treasures, not trash; jewels, not junk; good things, not garbage. That is the rule for the Give Away box.

Throw away things that are no good for you or others. Throw away false guilt, hurts, forgiven sins, arrogance, selfishness, and anger. And, please, no digging in the trash!

Finally, keep God's Word in your heart, mind, and memory. Hiding it in your heart will help you not sin against God. Having His Word in the Keep Box will also be a source of encouragement for you. Remember the words of Philippians 4:8 and the wonderful things we can keep and think on.

And when you get it clean, keep it clean. Remember Zacchaeus' example of handling the clutter so freely offered by the world and take it straight to the top. Refrain from addressing those who mutter at you. The Lord will help you so that you do not throw out something that you need or keep garbage that you'll trip over until next year when you dejunk again.

Your Choice

How have you done at spring cleaning your heart? Sorting through the stuff in your heart, mind, and memory is a choice. No one can force you to do it. No one can order you to be honest with yourself as you sort and sift the clutter.

It is your choice whether to give away treasures or trash. It is your choice whether or not to dig in the trash. And it is your choice whether you make the effort to keep it clean.

God will not force you either. He will, however, equip you for the task and encourage you in the process. His Word and the record of His work in people through the centuries assure us of this. May your heart be clean and committed to God—in spring and every season!

You may contact Kendra Smiley at:

Kendra Smiley
P.O. Box 104
East Lynn, IL 60932

ALSO AVAILABLE FROM THE AUTHOR:

Empowered by Choice!
Positive Decisions Every Woman Can Make

How can you take charge of your life? With compassionate insight, wisdom, and humor, Kendra Smiley motivates Christian women to live by their faith in all circumstances, telling true story after true story of women who have risen above great difficulties by making godly, positive choices. *Empowered by Choice* offers a proven recipe for confident living.

$10.99, 220 pages, paperback

Available at your local Christian bookstore
or from Servant Publications
P.O. Box 8617, Ann Arbor, MI 48107

Please include payment plus $3.25 per book
for shipping and handling.